Early Reviewer Praise for *Forever Green*

"*Forever Green* is a book that is '...a rich stew of imaginative stories, political commentary and original poems.' An aspect of the book that I particularly like is that the author is passionate about his beliefs, but he is gentle in presenting them. [Liam] states the premise of the book is Ireland's golden heritage and the flexibility of its people are, and will continue to, make the future one of hope and optimism. There are many parts of the book I like, but the strongest chapter, and the one I like the most, is the chapter called The Irish Rebel [in which he] tells the story of the 1916 Rebellion. [*Forever Green*] inspires us to hope for a peaceful, united Ireland. As Cathal Liam says in the last two sentences of the book '...help us deliver a nation of peace to the children of our tomorrow. They and Ireland deserve nothing less.'"
—Frank West, *The Irish American News*, (Chicago, IL)

"The dream of a free and united Ireland continues to haunt the Irish at home, as well as expatriates such as this Cincinnati author. Bookended by the 1916 rebellion and the Good Friday Accord of 1998, this collection of anecdotes, travel narratives, Irish poetry and excerpts from Liam's novel *Consumed In Freedom's Flame* is a reminder of the difficulty in bringing peace to a land rife with distrust."
—Rob Stout, *The Cincinnati Enquirer* (Cincinnati, OH)

"Cincinnati-based author Cathal Liam follows up his novel, *Consumed In Freedom's Flame*, with this collection of commentaries on Ireland's progress through the 20th century from 1916 up to the signing of the Good Friday agreement. Subtitled *Ireland Now & Again*, Liam's paperback includes an introduction from popular Irish landscape artist Edmund Sullivan and in a commentary on the back cover, journalist and author Terry Golway describes *Forever Green* as 'a wonderful, rollicking and passionate journey through the soul of Ireland and Irish-America.'"
—*The Irish Echo* (New York, NY)

"Subtitled *Ireland Now & Again*, Cathal Liam's book looks both backwards and forwards, back to an Ireland of heroic rebellion and sectarian strife, an Ireland of turf fires and traditional values, and forward to an Ireland where old shops have been replaced by 'plastic' pubs, where cooperation between the two factions in the North may eventually lead to the full implementation of the Good Friday Agreement. The collection of essays and poems would seem to be aimed primarily at an Irish American audience, and Mr. Liam does a good job in explaining the ongoing difficulties with the peace process. [He] has a commendable grasp of the events of the past five years in the North as well as an obvious love for Ireland which emerges in his descriptions of Galway City, of Croagh Patrick and of a day on the bog in the Irish midlands."
—Pauline Ferrie, *The Irish Emigrant (Galway, Ireland)*

Also by Cathal Liam

Consumed in Freedom's Flame:
A Novel of Ireland's Struggle for Freedom 1916-1921

FOREVER GREEN

IRELAND NOW & AGAIN

CATHAL LIAM

Introduction by the Irish-American Artist

EDMUND SULLIVAN

To the Fitzgeralds -
May the spirit of Ireland bloom in your hearts - always.
Cathal Liam
2004.

St. Padraic Press

This book is a rich stew of imaginative stories, political commentary and original poems. All of the affirmations and remembrances are the personal expressions of the author. Some of the narratives have been gently altered to mask the identity of persons living and dead.

Please note: Regarding Irish words used in this text, the sineadh fada notation over the appropriate vowel has been purposely omitted. This was done for simplicity and ease of manuscript preparation.

Printed in the United States of America
Text and cover design and production by Bookwrights Design
Cover painting by Edmund Sullivan
Back cover photo by Cathal Liam

First Edition
10   9   8   7   6   5   4   3   2

International Standard Book Number: 0-9704155-4-0
Library of Congress Card Number: 2003100577

Published by
St. Padraic Press
P.O. Box 43351
Cincinnati, Ohio 45243-0351 USA
For further inquiries: *www.cathalliam.com*

In memory of my dear parents...God rest their souls...

INTRODUCTION

"All great landscape painters have been dreamers."

—Duncan Phillips

Ireland has touched Cathal Liam, just as it has me. His thoughts and stories in this volume, *FOREVER GREEN: Ireland Now & Again*, evoke many of the same feelings and images that I try to convey in my paintings. As an Irish-American artist, one who has been profoundly influenced by the history and beauty of Ireland, his words touch my soul. They represent a link connecting the past to the present. They stir me, helping me recall my own roots, just as I imagine they will for those readers who are Irish too. I share Cathal's hope that together our words and my artwork become a celebration of Irish hearts, minds and souls, joined together in a tribute of who we are and what we all have in common.

Years ago, when I first began visiting Ireland, overwhelmed as so many of us are upon first seeing the magnificence of our ancestors' land, I wrote:

> Thousands of years have I stood eternally gazing upon thy beauty. I was exposed always to the sky and rain and mist, to the hill and vale and stream. I have been here and left aeons ago only to find you now again still wearing the bloom of youth.

So many things I have written, as I've roamed Ireland painting—wandering some thirty years and forty-four thousand miles to be exact. Inspired always by the gifts of love and fierce devotion to this Land of the Ancients.

My father was a Kerryman. He was too young to strike for Irish freedom in 1916. Six years later, however, he was a part of Ireland's bitter Civil War before leaving Munster to make a new life in America.

> Down a winding path, past stone ditches and nettle, over the gentle field and beyond. Step upon step, a strong step indeed toward the blue shadowed mountain and a lonely whitewashed farm. The spirit of those hills still takes residence, waiting for me, my father's son. I have walked under its brace and felt the echoes of long past. I've heard the tales and songs of yore. I have done the deed these thirty years. I've released your spirit and the lifeblood continues on into other times and times beyond these.

My father was a young man when he left his mountain home in 1926, never to walk Ireland's hills again. Some fifty-five years passed before that eternal spirit of an old man's youth crept up and took hold of my own. I then embarked upon my own Irish journey.

> Come, come it said, whispering softly, come. Gardens are blooming in all sorts of nooks and hollows. Roam these ancient hills as I did. I recall the once strong and young man or did I just dream a lovely dream?

My mother, born in Derry, was another driving force in my life. It was she who sparked my interest in painting, encouraged my sketching from the very beginning. Mom also gave me trust and a faith in God, yet never forsaking her fierce Irish-patriot heart. She even named me after a man, a brave sixteenth-century Jesuit theologian, who was hanged, drawn and quartered by the English: St. Edmund Campion. This book helps me remember him and the countless other

Irishmen and women who lived and died so one day Ireland might be free.

Some of the writing I have done echoes the words on Cathal's pages. I think all Irishmen and women feel it. Though different, they encapsulate versions of the same theme: Ireland, oh Ireland...Ireland, oh Ireland.... and everyone fits in the words to the rest of it, each according to their own perception of that beauty, of that terrible hunger to be free. They dream of their own wonderful earthly paradise until they can go home again. Home once more to refresh their aching memories of a long-lost but never forgotten Ireland.

The story of Father Michael Griffin brings those feelings to mind. He was part of that legion of men and women some of whom I have met over the years while painting Ireland. The countless individuals who have worked tirelessly for the virtue of 'Erin go braugh.' They possess brave, stalwart souls, brilliant souls, who fought in respectable, legal ways for the cause of Irish liberty. They have written editorials, published newspapers, staged raffles, organized dances, volunteered their time and raised millions of dollars in support of those who have been overwhelmed by 'the Troubles.' They and their efforts form a rich tapestry; a beautiful tapestry that is part of Ireland today. Yes, Father Griffin forfeited his life just as today others give up their time and resources for the same dream. By your reading, movie-going, supporting Irish causes, listening to the music, viewing the art, reciting the poetry, telling the stories and visiting Ireland you keep alive that spirit of freedom, unencumbered by outside forces who would wish to change Ireland into something it is not. In doing so, you become a part of it, just as I am through my painting and Cathal is through his writing.

After reading "The Pieces of Peace," I could not help but remember that I too was in Ireland in the summer of 1995. I had been painting very late into the evening. Finally, after loading up my car, I headed for Belfast. I needed to find a place to stay. As an Irish-American Catholic, I was aware that I had to select a part of town that would be safe for both my automobile and me. I stopped at several places, but feeling unsure of my surroundings, traveled on. Finally, I came upon two Royal Ulster Constabulary policemen. Though I remembered reading in the States how the RUC were often disliked by the Catholic-nationalist community in the North, the three of us had a lovely conversation. One of the policemen turned out to be a Protestant while the other was a Catholic. In the course of our conversation, the Protestant officer mentioned he was taking his family to the Irish Republic for a holiday. We all knew he was taking a chance doing so. If some paramilitary activists learned of this, the man might be in serious danger. Minutes later, as I drove off to their recommended hotel, I remember saying a prayer for that RUC man's safety. Though Ireland's eight-hundred-year history is a nightmare of sectarian division, I felt no animosity toward him. He was a genuine, warm human being. For a few brief moments, the three of us were brothers, brothers in God. I felt the oneness we had shared, and was glad I prayed for him and his family's safety.

There are many parallels between Cathal's writing and my painting. I could go on at length, but just one short story. I like to think of it as 'the day Michael Collins saved my life,' as there are several references to the 'Big Fellow' in the book. One summer's day, I was speeding along on a carriageway outside of Cork City heading for Kerry. I was doing over 80 mph, and foolishly was not wearing my seat belt. Suddenly, out of the corner of my eye a road sign flashed by. All it said was 'Site of Ambush.' I hit the brakes and quickly turned the car around. Though the sign offered absolutely no explanation as to its meaning, I intuitively knew what it meant. It pointed in the direction of an isolated spot, not far away, where Michael Collins was gun downed in 1922: Bealnablath! Back at the sign again, I turned off the main thoroughfare and headed up a narrow side road. It was rutted and full of potholes. I had only traveled a short way, when suddenly my front-right tire exploded. A massive blow-out that literally tore the rubber tubing apart. After coming to an abrupt stop, it suddenly occurred me. If I had been out on that motorway at 80 mph, I probably would be dead at this moment. Later, a garage mechanic confirmed that the punctured tire was without a doubt fatally flawed during manufacturing. So to this day, I firmly believe Michael Collins saved my life. When I finally have the chance to meet him up in Heaven, I will greet the 'Big Fellow' and slap him on the back saying, "Thank you for saving my life, Mick. Sure and thanks for giving me a few more years of life so I can continue doing things for the Irish people and have the pleasure of doing them as well."

A brief word about the painting on the front cover of this book. Much of my work is set on Ireland's west coast, spanning the northernmost to the southernmost landscapes. The mountains there afford me such visual power. They provide an overwhelming sense of timelessness of soul. I respond to it with charged emotion. This part of Ireland is an area full of artistic possibilities. The jagged resistance of the coastline with its smashing waves and dramatic weather changes calls to me. So I return there again and again.

I recognise distinctly different sides of my own nature. Because of this, I am also drawn to the stark beauty of the lonely landscapes: the bogs and the mist that enshrouds the harsh farming country toward which the Irish were pushed four hundred years ago. Melancholy, rocky and desolate, the mountains there pull me too. Connemara is such a place. Its absolute loneliness draws my soul, connects with my spirit. Though I choose not to return there often, its memory remains with me always. It is a great paradox and a very personal one. Perhaps this helps explain some of the subjects I select for my work.

While my paintings may be the final product, I empha-size that they are in fact only the medium. I do not dedicate my life to making pictures, but to opening pathways by which I, and those who view my work, might understand the deeper meanings expressed in my scenes. Thus, together we can con-nect with the driving force that first brought that expression to life. So the picture on this book's cover, like Cathal's words, is just a beginning: the starting point of a circle that ulti-mately brings us around, each to one another, as we seek eternal truths.

God bless each and every one of you. Together we are fellow spirits traveling the same road.

Edmund Sullivan
Sandy Hook, Connecticut
January, 2003
www.edmundsullivan.com

DANGEROUS DANCE...

By Peter O'Hanlon

Too long in trouble I wish it would end
Could we live side by side could we be friends?
We're not all the same I know this true
But I am just me and you are just you.

We tell our own lies relive our own past
The old dreams don't die the memories last
But to die for a dream is such a tragic romance
Prejudice and pride do a dangerous dance.

The best part of reason gets lost in time
The dust of old books is still in our eyes
And there's beauty in old books when there's
    truth on the page
And when we're all gone what will the books say?

Oh, hear the pipes play, take up your stance
And our children will pay
For our dangerous dance.

A WORD TO
THE READER...

I sat within the valley green,
I sat me with my true love;
My sad heart strove the two between,
The old love and the new love;
The old for her, the new that made
Me think of Ireland dearly,
While soft the wind blew down the glade,
And shook the golden barley.

The Wind That Shakes The Barley/Robert Dwyer Joyce

Forever Green: Ireland Now & Again is a collection of stories, assertions and poems about life, mostly the post-colonial years, in twentieth-century Ireland. As the title, *Forever Green* suggests, the affirmations and remembrances contained herein are incontrovertibly Irish in tone and intent. There is no question that they are inspired by the ancient dream of an Ireland free, united and independent...a country that can finally take its place among the nations of the earth.

The subtitle, *Now & Again*, has several connotations. There is the wistfulness of a fading culture, kept alive in the hearts and minds of romantics. These melancholy dreamers are the keepers of yesterday. In their minds, the hardships and troubles of the 'old days' are gone but not forgotten. What remains are the warmth and intimacy of a bygone era, whose mellow glow is reminiscent of a heavenly residue: the diffused remainder of sunset's fading light. But, lurking somewhere in the far corners of that yesterday, is the dark, bitter remembrance of betrayal and distrust. The rational mind tries to dismiss it, yet it lingers, refusing to die.

Now & Again also suggests a kind of nostalgia born of an Ireland in flux, struggling to find its place in our modern twenty-first-century world. Remembering bits of the old and apprehensive of the new, Ireland wants to change...to change for the better. However, Peter O'Hanlon's haunting words, *Too long in trouble I wish it would end...*cries out, as the past dies hard in Ireland...*and our children will pay for our dangerous dance.*

The title of the book in your hand also tries to capture the beauty and essence of Edmund Sullivan's wonderful paintings. The strong interplay of colour and light accentuate the beauty and simplicity of Ireland's rural countryside, so strikingly depicted on the book's cover. Appropriately, Mr. Sullivan entitles it simply "Ireland." Again, I thank Edmund for his wonderful contributions to this book.

If I might offer a suggestion...instead of reading this modest volume in a single go, digest it leisurely...maybe a story or two a day for a fortnight. Rather than polishing it off as you might typically do, I hope you would savour the stories, adding to each your own thoughts and musings. In doing so, the book becomes more of a personal excursion...a reflection of yesterday and an anticipation of tomorrow. To take a cue from what traditionally has been the Irish way: live life a bit more slowly...sure things will get done soon enough so. Remember, as some sage observed, "...it's the journey not the destination that makes all the difference...."

As you will soon discover, Irish history and politics are central themes running throughout the narrative. Their timelessness, often filled with a sense of frustration and despair, are counterbalanced by a newness, full of hope, for a better tomorrow. The Good Friday Agreement offers such a chance...an opportunity for peace, justice and a unity unknown in Ireland for a thousand years. It is a means to an end, like Michael Collins's stepping stones, rather than an end in and of itself. Additionally, the Belfast Accord's economic impact can be positive only when one considers the potential of the Irish people, working together, for the common good. There is still a long row to hoe, but just reflect on how far we have come in the last one hundred years.

Looking back, there have been two monumental bookend events in Ireland during that twentieth century: Dublin's Easter Rebellion in 1916 and the signing of Belfast's Good Friday Peace Accord in 1998. These watershed events have, and will continue to have, a lasting political, economic and social impact on the Irish world.

The 1916 Rising, led by Patrick Henry Pearse, James Connolly and a small cadre of other secessionists, had profound consequences. Initially, their effort to overthrow the might of the British government on Irish soil was crushed. Their hope of making a political statement to the world regarding Ireland's much-deserved independence was ignored. But from those ashes of defeat rose hope and a renewed resolve. Three years later, the Irish people were enmeshed in another deadly conflict: a war of independence. Though this contentious engagement produced no clear-cut victor, Ireland did gain a large measure of self-determination for twenty-six of its thirty-two counties. The Irish Free State was born. Later, it would become the parent of today's Irish Republic. Michael Collins and Eamon de Valera, opposing political giants, emerged from that morass. The personalities and deeds of these two men were destined to cast long shadows over Ireland. Indeed, they have.

Those turbulent years also spawned the seeds of further hatred and distrust. Ireland was partitioned by the British parliament in 1920, creating a satellite dependency known as Northern Ireland. In addition to this duplicitous legislation, Ireland's internal disagreement over British treaty terms tragically erupted into divisive civil war.

Finally, after decades of sporadic political and bitter sectarian confrontation, hope sprang anew with the signing of the 1998 Good Friday Peace Accord. Unfortunately, its expectations have yet to be realised. Sure the potential is there to sort out Ireland's differences in productive ways, but the human element in the equation is resistant. Years of hatred and distrust are deeply layered. More time and even greater tenacity are needed to strip away that veneer, exposing an unvarnished soul. The Irish people deserve no less. The watchwords 'peace with justice' must become reality. The ugliness that has so often reared its malevolent head must end. As the twenty-first century dawns, one can only hope that the Belfast Agreement will be a catalyst for positive change and significant good in Ireland's little corner of the world.

Several of the pieces in the book fit into the mould of travel narratives. They tend to be more 'off-the-beaten-track' anecdotes not found on your typical 'see-Ireland-in-a-week' tour. As you might already know or can easily imagine, Ireland is full of wonderful unexpected cubbyholes and crannies in addition to all its well-publicised tourist temptations. Whether you are wandering through an old graveyard looking for the headstone of a long-lost ancestor or enjoying a leisurely pony-and-trap excursion on Inishmore, Ireland is much more than just a Dublin pub crawl. Sure, if you only have a three-day weekend or the rest of your life, take time to taste and drink in the essence that is the Emerald Isle.

The stories, poems and commentaries found within are from the heart. If you enjoy them and agree with me, I am flattered. If not, well hopefully, I have caused you to contemplate and to examine what you believe to be so. As the Irish are great for saying, "Let us resolve our differences by agreeing to disagree." This world of ours would be a dull place if there were not some divergent thinking and differences of opinion to spice things up.

With regard to the political bits inside, I should warn you that it was never my intention to write a detailed review or comprehensive analysis of the last four or more decades with reference to Northern Ireland's 'Troubles.' I leave that task to other, more qualified, historians. But, I must mention that after living in the states for the last five years, much of the political reporting I have entertained has been through the filter of the American news media: a source which tends to be pro-British and anti-republican. (New York City's *Irish Echo* is the clear exception.) As a consequence, I readily admit that some of my commentaries are a reaction to those imperfect sources. I only hope my counterpoints fill the apparent gaps created by the political vacuums of those reports.

In conclusion, I sense there is a new day dawning in Ireland. Some welcome it with open arms, others do not. Regardless of your personal leanings, however, it is my fervent hope that all of us are the beneficiaries of that change and not its victims.

Cathal Liam
Cincinnati, Ohio
January, 2003
www.cathalliam.com

ACKNOWLEDGEMENTS...

I owe a big debt of thanks to many for their help in making this book possible. The ones that stand out include Turlough Breathnach; Beverly Bucannon & Danny Cummins; Madeline Bunt; David Burke, Editor, *Tuam Herald*; Michael Cadden; Francis Casey; Dr. Jim Coggan; Gabriel Cooley; Jim Cooney; Mary & Tom Corcoran; David Crowe; Dominic Delany; Kevin Donleavy; Dick Early; Krista & Pat Farrell; John M. Fitzgerald; Timothy Foote; Judy & Jon Griffin; Amy & Bob Harris; Mary Hayes, former Editor, *Midwest Irish News*; Dr. Ray Hebert; Leslie Huggard; Karin & Rich Jackoboice; Joe Keller; Mrs. Kenny, her sons and the staff of Kennys Bookshop; Mike Kull; Robert A. Mace, former Publisher, *Dream Weaver*; Connor Makem; Teddy & Sonny Malloy; Michael McCarthy; Tom Meehan; Mary Carol & John Melton; Father Francis Miller; Michael Murray; Ronnie O'Gorman, former Editor, *Galway Advertiser*; Ray O'Hanlon, Senior Editor, *The Irish Echo*; Albert O'Toole; May, Tim & Tom Richardson; Philip Thompson; Joann & Dr. Warren Van Zee; Dr. Tim White; Dr. Dean Wiles; Eileen & Tom Wright; Kate Wright; Richard Wright; Thomas Wright and my old friend #40, Jimmy 'Lamar' Wendell. Without their personal benevolence and writing encouragement I would have given up years ago.

Another assemblage of 'nameless' people to whom I owe a huge vote of thanks are all those good folks I have talked with at Irish/Celtic festivals around the United States. Their kind words, coupled with those of people I have met in bookstores, university classrooms, public libraries plus those who have written me mean so much. The welcoming encouragement I received from the book-reading public after the publication of my first novel, *Consumed in Freedom's Flame: A Novel of Ireland's Struggle for Freedom 1916-1921*, continues to sustain me.

A special word of indebtedness to Jack Cannon, Kevin Donleavy and Tony Gee for graciously reading and commenting on the manuscript. (The reading world anxiously awaits the publication of Kevin's new book, *Strings Of Life: Stories and Recollections of Old-Time Musicians from North Carolina and Virginia*, published this summer by Pocahontas Press of Blacksburg, Virginia.)

I am most grateful for the generous and thoughtful words of praise offered by the distinguished authors Terry Golway and Peter F. Stevens on behalf of the book. Their blurbs of endorsement are a proud and valued addition to it.

Additionally, may I extend my sincere appreciation to Tommy Makem (www.makem.com) and Peter O'Hanlon (www.bardis.ie) for the use of the lyrics to their inspiring songs.

My heartfelt thanks to Edmund Sullivan for writing the introduction to the book and for kindly contributing his artwork for the cover. Edmund's artistic talents are a brilliant addition to this project. I am most grateful.

Words seem so inadequate as I try expressing my 'thank you' to a great bird watcher and literary editor, Marcia Fairbanks. Her subtle wit, knowledge of writing and probing insights keep me well grounded and on my toes. She offers the perfect balance of sharp objectivity and gentle praise. She is someone I trust.

Everyone's contributions to the making of this book would be for nought if it were not for Mayapriya Long and Bookwrights Design. This talented woman has all the skills of a genius as she transforms typed pages on a computer disc into the printed words and cover of a book. It is an art few possess.

Acknowledgements...

Finally, my gratitude extends beyond the limits of my vocabulary as I thank my wife, Mary Ann, for putting up with my single-minded stubbornness. Her acceptance of my determined ways give meaning and fulfilment to my life. Her love and support nourish me.

01/01/01...

01/01/01...

This is a revision of an earlier piece I wrote in 1997 entitled "As Time Goes By." It appeared in the *Tuam Herald* (Tuam, Ireland) on 31 January 1998 under the title "Pondering Time." With the dawn of the new millennium, I made a few changes to my original story in late 2000...sure, I was just keeping up with the times.

01/01/01...Aye, triple ones! That certainly is a once-in-a-century occurrence. Indeed, some might even say a 'magical' date marked with special significance. Now at last, with the advent of the millennium just around the corner, thoughts of time and the calendar are raised to a higher level of consciousness. 'As time goes by...' 'Time flies when you are having fun...' 'Time marches on...' 'Time and tide for no man bide...' 'As ageless as time....' 'Time on your hands...' 'Time stands still...' 'Time out...' These everyday phrases are but a few of the many token expressions frequently offered up to 'the deity of time' who rules our lives with such exactness. So, on the dawning of a new century, 1 January 2001, the world will mark yet another momentous milestone in the passage of time.

Back home in Galway, Ireland, the long fascination with time is much in evidence, where the gable-end clock in William Street still proudly displays its 'Dublin time.' This great timepiece is a gentle reminder to all of the days when the Irish-capital trains first came to the west of Ireland. Back in the mid-nineteenth century Galway and Dublin were in different time zones. According to the rail timetable, the two towns were twenty minutes apart while London was a further twenty-five minutes ahead of the city by the River Liffey. The gable clock reminded everyone in Galway when the trains would arrive or depart via Dublin time, not local time.

There are other reminders of 'the good olde days' in this world of ours. For instance, in the Shetland Islands, situated to the north of Scotland's mainland, some of its residents continue to celebrate Christmas on January 5th and the New Year on the 12th. This curious custom reflects the continued use of the old Julian calendar that most of the world modified in 1582, but which oddly enough, Britain refused to adopt until 1752. It seems as though some Shetlanders still prefer remembering time as it was.

As we reminisce about the year gone by while looking forward to the next, most folks observe the timeless custom of hanging a new wall calendar that will grace our office or kitchen wall for the next twelve months.

Surprisingly, if truth were known, our modern timetable of today had its origins back in 46 B.C. when Julius Caesar established his new solar calendar. Each year had twelve months totalling 365 days. To every fourth year, however, he added an extra day to compensate for the earth's slightly irregular orbital path around the sun. Caesar's months alternated in length between thirty and thirty-one with the exception that the last month of the year, then February, was assigned only twenty-nine days in ordinary years. To bring things into proper balance, he added one day every fourth year to February. These special years eventually became known as Leap Years. To honour its creator, July was named for Julius.

Some time later, the grandnephew of Julius Caesar, Caesar Augustus, altered his great-uncle's design. Not only did he name the eighth month after himself, but also in a further effort to equalise matters, Augustus took one day from February and assigned it to August, which originally was only thirty days long. As a result, February would forever have twenty-eight days in ordinary years and twenty-nine in Leap Years.

Unfortunately, Julius Caesar's astronomers made a slight error in their solar measurements. Each year's actual length was miscalculated by eleven minutes and fourteen seconds. As a result, by the time the sixteenth century rolled around, the cumulative mistake totalled ten days.

In an effort to correct this miscue, Pope Gregory XIII in 1582 decreed that October 5th would become October 15th. (It seems that popes in former times had considerably more power and influence than they do today!) Additionally, aided by new scientific understandings, Gregory fine-tuned his calendar by ordaining that centuried years such as 1600, 1700, 1800, etc. would not be designated as Leap Years unless they were evenly divisible by four hundred.

Regrettably for those living in the British Isles and Ireland, England's Protestant monarch, Elizabeth I, refused to accept the Catholic pope's calendar adjustments. As you can imagine, this decision caused great confusion between English and Continental calendars for many years to come.

Finally in 1750, fuelled by the growing disparity between the Julian and Gregorian calendars, the British parliament decided to act. They declared that 2 September 1752 would become 14 September. (As you can see, with the passage of more time Caesar's original error had grown even larger.) England's ruling body also changed the first day of the year from 25 March to 1 January. By doing so, British and European calendars were at last brought into harmony with one another. If this singular change had not occurred, 24 March 1752 would have been followed by 25 March 1753. (The date, 25 March, still marks the advent of Britain's fiscal year.)

This change also explains why, according to the old English calendar, the Battle of the Boyne was fought on 1 July 1690 O.S., meaning Old Style, and why William III's victory over James II is celebrated, at least in some parts of Ireland, as if it had occurred on 12 July.

Ah well, time does have a way of sorting things out. Just think back several years ago when everyone was consumed with the pressing need to program his or her computer to deal with the dreaded 'double zero' dilemma.

So, on that memorable note, whether in Old Style or in New, Julian or Gregorian, many happy returns of the New Year.

DUBLIN'S
SAINT VALENTINE...

DUBLIN'S SAINT VALENTINE...

About a decade ago, as I wandered through the narrow streets behind Dublin Castle, the former seat of British authority in Ireland, I intentionally walked past the corner of Bishop Street and Peter Lane. Dublin Corporation workers were knocking down the last bits of the main section of Jacob's Biscuit Factory. Its buildings had been unoccupied since the late 1970s or early 1980s. Not surprisingly, during the next ten years the complex had become derelict: a vandalised cluster of buildings that were a neighbourhood eyesore.

Today, the main factory site serves as the home to Dublin's Institute of Technology. Its concrete and glass architecture, however, bears no resemblance to its location's former occupant. In deference to the old, however, some of the original granite stonework is visible along the upper floors, especially down the Peter Lane expanse. Behind the vocational school, some of the old structures have been renovated and serve as a central repository for Ireland's historical archives.

Back in 1916, Jacob's, maker of 'sweet' biscuits and one of Dublin's few major employers, was one of the principal spots occupied by Irish revolutionary forces. These military secessionists were seeking Ireland's independence from England's centuries-old domination.

The former bakery's imposing triangular-shaped facade looked out on one of Dublin's major north-south thoroughfares, Aungier Street, hard by a modest incline known as Redmond's Hill. It was an ideal defensive location. Situated amid a warren of narrow streets, lined with small dwellings, the factory's sturdy stone walls and sheltered location made it virtually resistant to enemy counter-attack.

Almost a century ago, the now-demolished building served as headquarters for Irish Volunteer Commander Thomas MacDonagh's Second Battalion. Jacob's tall twin towers loomed over south Dublin. Inside its stout perimeter, the teacher who had recently become a rebel military officer directed a force of approximately one hundred and fifty men. From the Castle on its north, to the two British military barracks located just beyond the Grand Canal to its south, any carelessly exposed British soldier would have been in grave danger of being shot by rebel sharpshooters stationed on the building's lofty heights.

But that was then, this is now. Heading back down Aungier Street toward the River Liffey, I passed an unpretentious building advertising itself as Whitefriar Street Carmelite Church. Pausing before its doorway, I recalled an old Irish expression, "Just imagine, I wasn't in a church today!" Realising those words applied to me, I decided to go inside, say a prayer, light a candle and have a look around.

Located just one block north of MacDonagh's former Easter Rebellion HQ, the church was unlike most churches in Ireland. Its stubby narthex looked more like the entrance to an office building than a church.

I headed up a slight terrazzo incline toward the back of the hallway. To the left was a small religious book and retail shop, while straight on was the actual entrance to the nave. Its interior was candle-lit and surprisingly spacious. It reminded me more of an assembly hall than a church. Its side aisles were punctuated by a series of small chapels and shrines, also aglow with holy illuminations.

Imagine my surprise when I discovered that one of those memorials was dedicated to Saint Valentine. There, in a carved niche in the wall, stood a large statue of the patron saint of lovers. A notation on the altar stated that the remains of the man himself were enshrined in the coffin just beneath the marble slab. (Valentine is also the patron saint of epileptics. A disease from which he supposedly suffered.)

Later, as I left the church, I vowed to look into this matter further. The following represents the results of that inquiry. It is a written revision of a presentation I made several years ago on Saint

Valentine and how his final resting place happens to be in Dublin, Ireland.

DUBLIN'S SAINT VALENTINE…It is hard to imagine that the remains of Saint Valentine, the patron saint of lovers, now reside in a small neighbourhood church in the heart of Dublin, Ireland. But this appears to be the case. How did it happen? This is what I discovered.

The Whitefriar Street Carmelite Church at #57 Aungier Street is tucked away behind a modest facade on a busy south Dublin street. The building's unusual design seems to owe itself to the cramped space it occupies. Now wedged in among shops and small houses, the church resides on the site of a former pre-Reformation Carmelite priory built in 1539. Fate was unkind to the old structure. Today, nothing remains of the previous construction. In its place is a Carmelite church dating from the 1820s. Its cornerstone, laid in 1825, is the handiwork of architect George Papworth (1781-1855). [Mr. Papworth was a well-known Dublin designer who, it was believed, also designed the city's St. Mary's Pro-Cathedral, dedicated in 1825. St. Mary's is Dublin's foremost Catholic church despite its being located on a narrow back street just to the east of O'Connell Street. It originally was to be built on the city's main thoroughfare, Sackville (now O'Connell) Street, but the town's Anglo-Irish leadership vetoed that idea. Instead, St. Mary's construction was relegated to obscurity on Marlborough Street while the impressive General Post Office building was erected on its intended location facing Europe's widest avenue.]

Unlike two of Dublin's famous tourist attractions, Christ Church Cathedral and St. Patrick's Cathedral, both of which are Protestant or Church of Ireland in denomination, this unassuming Carmelite church is Catholic and a beloved neighbourhood house of worship.

Besides its tribute to Saint Valentine, Whitefriar's has two other interesting appeals. Not far from Saint Valentine's shrine is an elaborate altar above which a Flemish oak statue of the Virgin and Child resides. This late fifteenth or early sixteenth-century sculpture was thought to have once belonged in St. Mary's Abbey on Dublin's north side. What makes this wooden carving so special is that it is believed to be the only remaining artefact to escape the ravages wrought by the English crown's annihilation of Ireland's monasteries during the Reformation. By the grace of God and the efforts of some unknown dedicated souls, the statue somehow survived despite the abbey's destruction.

Also in this same church is Saint Albert's Well. On his feast day, August 7th, a relic of this thirteenth-century disciple of God, St. Albert or Albertus Magnus, is dipped in the sacred fount. All blessing themselves with this holy water are reportedly granted both physical as well as spiritual healing.

Returning to the matter at hand, who was Saint Valentine and how did his remains end up in the heart of Dublin Town?

The *Catholic Encyclopedia* states that there were at least three different Saint Valentines. "...all three of them are mentioned in the early martyrologies under the date of 14 February." One was thought to have been a priest in Rome, another a bishop in Interamna (now Terni, Italy) and a third, who suffered in Africa with a number of companions. Little is known of this last martyr.

Whether the priest and bishop were actually two distinct individuals or not, time and myth seem to have fused their accomplishments, creating a solitary figure dedicated to the commemoration of lovers. Valentine or Valentinus, as he was probably known in Latin, lived in Italy during the third century. From all accounts, this man was certainly devoted to God and Christianity.

His troubles began in 269 A.D. when Emperor Claudius II decided single men made better soldiers for his legions than did married or family men. His conclusion was based on the fact that military enlistments had recently fallen off. Betrothed men were refusing to join the emperor's army. To counter this growing problem, Claudius II forbade all young men to marry. Valentine refused to obey his sovereign's unfair decree. Realising the danger in which he must be placing himself, Valentine continued to wed couples, albeit secretly, while, I assume, he performed other acts of Christian charity.

Maybe it was this act of royal betrayal, or the possibility that Valentine had helped fellow Christians escape from Roman prisons where inmates were frequently beaten and tortured, or both, but his criminal behaviour certainly became known to Claudius. The emperor ordered the man arrested and put to death.

While he was incarcerated, Valentine's friends and followers 'supposedly' threw notes and flowers through a window into his cell. Legend also tells us that the youthful priest fell in love with the jailer's daughter, who frequently visited him in prison. Some accounts even have Valentine curing the young woman of her blindness. In any event, on the day he was clubbed to death and beheaded (14 February 269), the prisoner allegedly penned a letter to his love, signing it "...from your Valentine." Afterwards, he was buried on the Flaminian Way near the ancient Flaminian Gate. In a short time, this entranceway into Rome became known as the Gate of St. Valentine (now the Porta del Popolo).

The real truth behind the Valentine legend is lost in time. But the portrayal of this young man, dedicated to his Christian faith, makes him an appealing heroic figure, full of sympathetic and amorous nuances. It is easy to understand how the theme of love grew, enveloping Valentine: a life of love with its romantic overtones and now worldly traditions.

Valentine's story is also entwined with pagan and Christian mythology. During mid-February, two pagan festivals were annually held in Rome. On the 14th, a special social affair was held for Juno, the Goddess of women and marriage. On the following day, the 15th, the Feast of Lupercalia, when birds were thought to begin their spring mating, began. Custom had it that on the eve of Lupercalia, young unmarried men would draw the name of an adolescent woman from a vessel. This new couple would be partnered for the remainder of the celebration. Occasionally, this chance pairing even ended in marriage.

Later, the leadership of the early Christian church wanted to purge the idolatrous elements from all festivals. It began substituting the names of saints for those of pagan deities. This was the fate that Lupercus, the god of fertility and sexual pleasure, encountered at the end of the fifth century. Pope Gelasius I (d. 496 A.D.), wishing to substitute a holy figure for the sinful icon, selected Saint Valentine as the focus for that traditional springtime celebration. Since the Lupercian gala was held in the middle of February, it was understandable why Gelasius renamed it in honour of Valentine. It is also likely that the act of choosing a person to be your valentine, or a saint to be your patron, originated from these early Christian times.

Finally, I give you a few heartfelt, springtime beliefs and customs worthy of note:

- The first flower of the spring, the crocus, has become known as Saint Valentine's flower.
- In the middle ages, young men and women would draw the names of their valentines from a bowl. They would then wear that person's name on their sleeve. From that tradition grew the saying, "wearing your heart on your sleeve," as an expression of openly showing your emotions.

- In Wales, wooden love spoons were carved and given as gifts on February 14th.
- Some believe that if a woman sees a robin on Saint Valentine's Day, she will marry a sailor. If she sees a sparrow, she will marry a poor man but be happy. If it is a goldfinch she spots, she will marry into wealth.
- Of course, the present-day custom of exchanging cards and flowers might easily stem from the gifts Valentine received from his admirers while in prison almost two thousand years ago. Giving sweets to your sweetheart is a natural extension of those acts of caring and kindness.

Well, after all this, what is the Dublin connexion? It seems that Pope Gregory XVI presented the recently consecrated Whitefriar's church with the remains of Saint Valentine to honour and to recognise the great humanitarian work carried out by its Prior, Father John Spratt. His reputation as a tireless worker and champion of the poor in Dublin was well known throughout Ireland and in Rome. Thus, in 1835, as Fr. Spratt was on a lecture tour in The City of Seven Hills, he was invited to attend a special audience with the Pope. As part of that holy meeting, Gregory XVI presented Prior Spratt with the recently exhumed remains of the saint, who had for centuries been buried in Rome's St. Hippolyus Cemetery. Finally, on 10 November 1836, a casket containing Saint Valentine's remains and a holy chalice tinged with his blood were enshrined in Dublin's Carmelite church.

So, the next time you are in Dublin, take a few minutes of your stay and visit the little Whitefriar's Church on Aungier Street. As you step inside its quiet, peaceful walls, walk down the aisle and look to your right. Saint Valentine's chapel welcomes you. Walk over and say a prayer or two in his honour. You just never know...you may be surprised to discover a little more 'love' has crept into your heart.

THE OLDEST
BUILDING IN
GALWAY...

THE OLDEST BUILDING
IN GALWAY...

After learning of this architectural find in early January, 1998, I spent several days visiting the site and talking with Michael Murray, Galway's Collector of Customs & Excise; Dominic Delany, Director of Excavations; and Michael Cadden, Office of Public Works architect. This story could not have been written without their kind help. To my pleasure, the piece was published in the March, 2002 issue of the *Midwest Irish News* (Columbus, Ohio).

THE OLDEST BUILDING IN GALWAY...Galway, Ireland, now a popular tourist destination, was once a wealthy medieval city. Rich in history, today's burgeoning municipality is liberally sprinkled with centuries-old buildings, proudly awaiting the eager photography enthusiast.

Recently, its architectural wealth was enhanced by a remarkable discovery. On your next visit to 'the City of Tribes,' stroll down Flood Street. As you pass by the Custom House door, pause and listen carefully. Maybe, just maybe, you will hear the French-speaking Richard De Burgo, nicknamed the Red Earl, and his Anglo-Norman clansmen, raising their voices in song while they hoist their ancient goblets filled with mead. For once again to the delight of many, more of Galway's history has been uncovered.

Tucked away in a small courtyard, surrounded by a redbrick building housing the city's custom and excise offices, is an extraordinary archaeological find. Unearthed by accident, when Custom House expansion began, are the partial remains of a thirteenth-century medieval hall. This remarkable find marks the oldest, and some say, the most significant architectural discovery from Galway's storied past.

According to historical records, this ancient site once housed the De Burgos' medieval hall. Civic events and 'lavish' banquets would have been held there, and possibly, the Red Earl himself (d. 1326) could have held court within its walls while imposing his own brand of justice on those he ruled. (A number of similar ancient hall-keeps have been unearthed in Britain, but very few have been discovered in Ireland. This fact only enhances the importance and significance of this unique Galway find.)

Prior to the beginning of construction on the Custom House addition, a site survey, required by Irish law, was undertaken. It was during this period of testing that the remains of a medieval stone structure came to light. After consultation of old city maps and preserved town documents, the connexion between the De Burgos and the newly discovered ruin was made.

From a historical viewpoint, records indicate that in 1185 William De Burgo, an Anglo-Norman from Wales, joined in the early exploitation of Ireland begun in 1169 with the arrival of Robert Fitzstephen, Richard Fitzgilbert de Clare (Strongbow) and others. William's son, Richard, had his eye set on the west of Ireland. So in 1232, he led an impressive array of knights, soldiers, archers and civilian opportunists across the River Shannon ford at present-day Athlone. He divided up his purloined land, giving some of it to his friends. Astutely, however, he established his own royal residence on a narrow peninsula of dry high ground where Galway City stands today. No doubt, it was Richard or his son Walter who selected the site on which to build their new meeting hall. Interestingly enough, the place chosen was the same spot that for centuries the ancient Irish Connacht men had used to erect their own primitive duns or forts. (Close examination of Galway's famous 1651 pictorial map clearly shows the partial ruins of the hall, named for Walter's son Richard, the Red Earl, but incorrectly identified as a castle.)

To date archaeologists have made many splendid discoveries at the site. The presently exposed ruin reveals what once was a single-story, one-room building whose walls were almost three feet thick. They were made of loose native stones mortared together to hold them in place. These outer parapets, approximately ten feet high, were supported by a series of stone buttresses. These walls contained two opposing doorways, each featuring dressed limestone jamb stones. The hall's interior dimensions measured roughly twenty by sixty feet.

No evidence of roofing material exists today, but an educated guess would conclude that it was probably made of wood and native thatching. It seems likely that the De Burgos occupied this hall for about two hundred years...from the late 1200s to the late 1400s.

Sometime in the fourteenth or fifteenth century the building underwent extensive renovation. A series of octagonal, dressed limestone columns was erected down the centre of the building, no doubt further reinforcing the roof. During this later period of refurbishment, at least one of the original doorways was altered, as a second phase of buttressing was undertaken. In addition to its ancient walls and columns, the dig team has unearthed quantities of copper artefacts and numerous pottery chards including imported French and Portuguese wares.

Gradually, the De Burgos' reign came to an end as political and religious forces shifted in the growing town. In 1484, Galway officially gained a great measure of self-determination from the English crown when King Richard III granted it a Royal Charter. In the same year Pope Innocent VIII bestowed collegiate status upon its Church of Saint Nicholas. As a result, Galway Town gained much secular and religious independence from its former overseers while the De Burgos' unquestioned authority and influence began to wane.

The political and economic vacuum created by one family's declining fortunes was filled by the rising prosperity of fourteen other clans. Known as the Fourteen Tribes of Galway, these powerful merchant families propelled Galway, a newly flourishing 'city-state,' into the economic forefront as a major trading centre. For two hundred years, Galway Town was England's third most important port after London and Bristol.

To support this notion of De Burgo family decline, unearthed archaeological evidence indicates the now abandoned hall was reused as an iron workshop in the sixteenth century. This industrial activity appears to have continued into the early 1600s. Of special interest was the discovery of a section of late-medieval courtyard built on the southwest side of the old building. Its surface was paved with large cobblestones and contained a well-defined drain that ran along its rough surface.

During the sixteenth and seventeenth centuries, the longstanding structure underwent even more modifications. The western-most doorway was enclosed, the courtyard drain was paved over and two stone-lined rubbish pits were dug along the hall's southwest corner. Used by the surrounding residents, these post-medieval garbage dumps have yielded a substantial quantity of artefacts including broken pottery vessels, clay pipes, glass goblets, wine bottles and various metal objects.

Years later, the old hall cum foundry must have been knocked down and a more 'modern-day' edifice erected in its place. This new structure may have served for a time as a courthouse because the neighbouring laneway was formerly called Courthouse Lane. Today, this same passageway is called Druid Lane in honour of the little theatre now gracing its footpath.

Finally, a word about today's Custom House completes this saga. The present redbrick building on Flood Street was built in the mid-1940s. Behind it and to the west of the medieval hall is an early nineteenth-century warehouse with a late-1800 addition appended to it. These structures were used to store spirits and tobacco imported into Galway back in those days.

Presently, the ancient hall's archaeological excavation is finished, but the further identifying, dating and piecing together of its uncovered artefacts continues. Plans are under way to incorporate the existing stone walls of the old De Burgo hall and paved courtyard of the ironworks into part of the new Custom House addition. Together, they will serve as wonderful backdrops for exhibiting the newly unearthed treasures found nearby. To the delight of many, the hall's ancient stone walls and once-buried relics will be displayed for the entire world to see, study and appreciate.

THE MYTH & MYSTERY OF SAINT PATRICK REVISITED...

THE MYTH & MYSTERY OF SAINT PATRICK REVISITED...

The following first appeared in print in 1998, inspired by a shorter piece composed a year earlier. As with everything I write, it has been revised several times. Over the past five years, parts of the story have appeared in *The Daily Progress* (Charlottesville, Virginia), *Galway Advertiser* (Galway, Ireland), and *Midwest Irish News* (Columbus, Ohio).

THE MYTH & MYSTERY OF SAINT PATRICK REVISITED...A year ago, as I trudged up the rough pathway leading to the top of Croagh Padraic (Co. Mayo), my thoughts filled with the dramatic and tragic events that for centuries have gripped this historic land stretched out before me.

For aeons, legend has ascertained it was on this Irish mountaintop, sometime in the mid-fifth century, that Ireland's patron saint, Patrick, paid his Lenten devotions to God and Christ. 'Tis also reported that the man himself banished the island's snakes from these same lofty heights that bear his name today.

As Ireland's national day (17 March) once again drew nigh, I remembered looking with hungry eyes to the hills and mountains around Clew Bay...from the Twelve Pins to Slievemore...for a glimpse of a new 'modern-day' Saint Patrick. I eagerly sought someone who could peacefully dissolve the age-old tensions of nationalist and unionist discord that still trouble Ireland's tortured breast.

As my eyes searched the green and rocky countryside, I wondered if my pagan ancestors hungrily welcomed 'Patrick the Briton' in his day as do those who now seek conciliation and compromise from that same quarter (Britain).

History notes that the conversion of Emperor Constantine to the Christian religion in 312 A.D. quickened its growth, but its evolution over the next two hundred years was slow and uneven. By the end of the fifth century, only an estimated five million acknowledged believers could be counted.

Of that Irish yesterday, there is no reliable documented evidence until the year c. 435 A.D. It was in the Prosper of Aquitaine's *Chronicle* that the world received its first written glimpse of Christianity on the Emerald Isle.

Christians, however, had been living in Ireland for some time. Many of these early believers were kidnapped and brought to the Holy Ground as prisoners of war from the land across the Irish Sea. Others, no doubt, were converts returning home after living for a time in Scotland, Wales or England. Thus, by the year 431 A.D., the number of 'new believers' must have been of sufficient magnitude to warrant Pope Celestine sending a bishop, a man of old Gallo-Roman aristocracy named Palladius. His charge was to oversee religious activities and assure obedience to the Christian doctrine of the time.

History chooses to forget Palladius's accomplishments. Instead, it focuses its attention on another Christian envoy by the name of Patrick. Over and above the admiration he deserves for his difficult mission in God's name, it was Patrick's two surviving writings, his *Confession* and *Letter*, that serve as our major source of insight into fifth-century Ireland. But just as today's written word is subject to revision, so too was Patrick's.

The earliest surviving manuscript containing the saint's words can be found in the *Book of Armagh* dated c. 807 A.D. But these ancient scholars did not balk at changing history to suit their own fancy while promoting their church as the island's primary religious centre of the day. Sadly, their censored version of Patrick coupled with the fact that he chose to write virtually nothing about himself, forever darkens our true understanding of who he was and how he lived his life. We do not even know the actual dates of his birth or death. His writings simply portray a man living on the edge of a Christian and pagan world. What is written of him, therefore, is regrettably only myth and fiction passed down from century to century by well-meaning people who had their own agenda to foster.

What we do know is that Patrick did not spread Catholicism. He simply sowed the seeds of Christianity among Gaelic pagans and nurtured the souls of his fellow believers. In reality, there was no 'Roman Catholic Church' per se in Ireland or elsewhere until the sixteenth-century Protestant Reformation. Aye, Saint Patrick did convert the Irish to Christianity, but in his day it was neither Catholic nor Protestant. As a result, the man belongs to all Irish and all Christians regardless of their doctrinal faith.

All this I thoughtfully contemplated, as I stared out toward the cliffs of Achill Island and the rolling Atlantic, while wistfully wishing for another 'Patrick' miracle.

Later that afternoon, on my return journey down the mountain, I suddenly remembered the youth group that several years ago performed a symbolic play in the nave of England's Lincoln Cathedral. This was not a typical biblical tale.

Instead, it was set in a post-apocalyptic world where people were dying of thirst. The performers wore gas masks, as their make-believe air was unfit for breathing. The main character, a messiah-like figure dressed in white, preached that their ancestors, residing in the earth below, must be reawakened so the soil could once again bloom and sustain life.

The performance was part of an ecumenical conference entitled *Earth Our Home* and was a blending of God and green...of giving depth and meaning to one's religion while focusing on the need for a greater understanding about our endangered environment.

Looking back on that morality play, I wondered if the men and women who climb Patrick's mountain today might somehow awaken the spirit of our long-dead Irish ancestors. Eagerly then, with the help of a 'new' Saint Patrick, each of us might sow the seeds of Christian understanding, of love for one another and of harmony with our world so that Ireland's green and orange no longer need be separated by the white....

ALBERT O'TOOLE: GALWAY'S FAMOUS WOODCHOPPER...

ALBERT O'TOOLE: GALWAY'S FAMOUS WOODCHOPPER...

Written in early 1998, this narrative first appeared in the *Tuam Herald* (Tuam, Ireland) on 31 October 1998. Later, the story was featured in the September, 2001 issue of the *Midwest Irish News* (Columbus, Ohio).

ALBERT O'TOOLE: GALWAY'S FAMOUS WOOD-CHOPPER...Today, residing on a quiet back street bordering Galway's once-busy, nineteenth-century Eglington Canal, lives a modest but proud man. This gifted sculptor took a God-given talent and, through hard work as well as long hours of loving dedication, perfected his skills. At long last, his woodcarving genius is being acknowledged in Ireland; but to the rest of the world, he is still a little-recognised artist.

Albert O'Toole, born in Galway just over three score years ago, prefers to think of himself as "just a simple woodchopper." But, after a moment's reflection from his parlour window, which looks out upon the now tranquil canal and its idle locks, you are quickly reminded that this is no ordinary man. No, this is the home of a gifted artist who possesses a unique aptitude.

Comfortably seated across from Albert, I immediately notice his sparkling eyes. Their warmth and brightness catch and hold my attention. I recall his handshake at the door was firm, alive and marked by a noticeable roughness. I remember thinking that this is the hand of someone seldom idle.

Glancing around the modest room, something else catches my eye. There on the wall next to the chimney is a face that is so familiar. It is half of the wooden mould that was used to form the silhouetted head of Irish-American John Fitzgerald Kennedy, America's thirty-fifth president. Sure, 'tis the very same bronze tribute now proudly on display in Galway's Eyre Square, just up the road from where I sit.

Yes, it is none other than Albert O'Toole, the man seated across from me, who fashioned, from a fine block of native Irish walnut, the striking die which produced the City of Tribes's famous Kennedy memorial.

Talking about his work, the soft-spoken Irishman describes how he discovered his unique talent. Trained as a joiner (furniture maker) in his youth, Albert decided, some forty years ago, to try his hand at woodworking to help pass the time one winter's night. Modifying a cutthroat razor to create a specialised carving knife, he took a block of wood and began copying a small plaster cast of Pope Pius XII. Several days later, he presented his family with a wooden figure that would make any master proud.

O'Toole, entirely self-taught, asserts, "It is better to do things on your own. My mind is always creating something. I gain great satisfaction knowing I use my own skills and talents rather than depending on someone else for ideas or techniques." Modestly, Albert stresses that he began his woodworking chiefly as a hobby and for relaxation.

I move to sit next to him on the sofa. The artist and I now slowly leaf through a scrapbook containing photographs of some of his favourite carvings. He points with satisfaction to his wooden figure of Saint Francis with Dove that today decorates an interior wall of Galway's Franciscan Abbey. Next the man talks of creating the thorn-crowned head of Christ which currently hangs in Galway's Mercy Convent school. Finally, Mr. O'Toole speaks of his striking Hand of the Crucified Christ that resides in a private home near Ennis Town in Co. Clare.

In addition to these individual carvings, the woodworking master quietly notes he has carved Stations of the Cross sets for several village churches in the west of Ireland including ones in Doolin, Kinvara and Craughwell. These gifts of artistic beauty will continue serving for years as lasting reminders of his special talents to the residents of those communities.

Later, enjoying a quiet pint in a local pub, O'Toole speaks briefly of former days when, as a member of the Galway Art Club, he displayed his work at their annual art shows. But, an immense feeling of pride radiates from the man when he talks of his involvement with the creation of the bas-relief, commemorative head of former President John Kennedy.

With the 1963 announcement of JFK's planned summer visit to Ireland and his scheduled arrival in Galway to receive its prized Freeman honour, Albert decided to carve a wooden silhouette of Kennedy's wife, Jackie, to mark the occasion. Unfortunately, the pregnant Mrs. Kennedy was unable to accompany her husband on the visit. But despite Albert's obvious disappointment, he did present his finished work to America's Irish Ambassador, Matt McCloskey. Upon seeing the carving, the politician remarked, "You've certainly captured the First Lady to perfection."

The following day, the artist and his proud wife, Maree, sat in an especially reserved section of Eyre Square and watched the American leader receive his coveted Irish title. Five months later, President Kennedy was dead: assassinated in Dallas, Texas.

The next two years passed quickly. Then, with the planned dedication of Galway's new cathedral by Boston's Richard

Cardinal Cushing, it was disclosed that the invited church leader would also rededicate the park in Eyre Square in honour of the murdered American president. Upon learning of this, Albert remembers telling his father that he would like to do another plaque...this time to honour JFK.

Soon afterwards, the elder O'Toole spoke with Galway's Mayor Paddy O'Flaherty about his son's interest. A few weeks later, the City Corporation agreed to have Albert carve the wooden mould that would serve as the pattern for the bronze bas-relief of Kennedy's head. The likeness was to be the centrepiece of Galway's enduring memorial to the late Irish-American president.

Finally, on 15 August 1965, in addition to blessing Galway's new cathedral, Cardinal Cushing renamed the grassy quadrangle in the centre of Eyre Square, Kennedy Park. On that day, Albert and his wife joined an assemblage of dignitaries on the ceremonial platform. Included on the dais were Irish President Eamon de Valera, Taoiseach (Prime Minister) Sean Lemass, Irish Primate Cardinal William Conway, Galway's Mayor Brendan Holland to mention a few.

As part of the dedication ceremony, Albert O'Toole's silhouette of John F. Kennedy, nobly affixed to a huge slab of locally quarried Galway limestone, was unveiled for all the world to see. Of that day, Albert remembers Cardinal Cushing's words upon first seeing the product of the artist's handiwork, "What a wonderful likeness of JFK that is."

Today, his beautifully carved wooden mould hangs in the O'Toole home, while the bronze bas-relief resides with understated dignity behind the Quincentennial Fountain in Kennedy Park in the centre of Eyre Square.

So as thousands of foreign visitors and local residents pause before that monument each year, Galwegians can take great pride in knowing that one of Ireland's most talented artist lives and works among them...a man of modest means who describes himself as just a 'simple woodchopper.'

THE PIECES
OF PEACE...

THE PIECES OF PEACE...

On 31 August 1994, the Provisional Irish Republican Army announced that, as of midnight, it was calling a cease-fire. All units were instructed to lay down their arms in a show of support for the ongoing Northern Irish peace process. (Note: In 1969, the newly-erupted violence in Northern Ireland became an upsetting catalyst. The ranks of the Irish Republican Army split. Opposed to the organisation's growing socialist tendencies and its recent interest in joining Ireland's established political process, some time-honoured militarists broke away from the main body. They renamed themselves the Provisional Irish Republican Army (PIRA) and were nicknamed the Provos. This new group, wanting nothing to do with traditional democratic politics, planned to drop the label 'provisional' from their name within the year. History notes, though, they never did. The left-leaning members of the IRA also adopted a new title, calling themselves the Official IRA. The Officials ultimately suspended military operations in 1972 while the Provos pursued their armed campaign. Initially, the PIRA took a defensive posture, protecting Catholics from the ravages of loyalist sectarian violence. Buoyed, however, by the addition of new recruits and with the increased backing of devoted followers, the Provos soon took the offensive. They planned to force the British Army out of Northern Ireland while hoping to finally unite their partitioned country. In keeping with an age-old political Irish tradition, some members of the Officials, unwilling to accept their group's cease-fire, broke away. They reorganised themselves, becoming the Irish National Liberation Army or INLA. Today, the labels PIRA and IRA refer to the same people and the same organisation.)

Less than two months later, on 13 October 1994, loyalist paramilitaries proclaimed their own cease-fire. Northern Ireland looked forward to peace. You could feel it in the air.

The following summer of 1995 was the first in decades when murder, mayhem and maliciousness were decidedly absent in the Six Counties. All Ireland rejoiced. Tourism and hope flourished throughout the island. Everyone breathed a collective sigh of relief, as both communities began enjoying the dividends of peace. All was not perfection, however. Life, especially in the North, reso- nated with sectarian stress and political pressure. Mercifully, though, the peace process continued limping along.

United States President Bill Clinton visited Ireland that De- cember. The following month, January, 1996, an international body headed by American Senator George Mitchell published its his- toric guidelines. It outlined the non-violent principles all political parties must adhere to before they could participate in all-party talks. Again, a new sense of optimism filled the air. Sadly, however, it was short-lived.

At six o'clock in the evening 9 February 1996, the Provisional IRA ended its ceasefire. It blamed British Prime Minister John Major and his government for allowing selfish party and sectarian interest to obscure the wants and desires of all Irish people. One hour later, a huge bomb was detonated in an underground garage of the Canary Wharf building in east London. Two people were killed and millions of pounds of damage were meted out to London's economy.

By the autumn of 1996, the IRA's strategy of wreaking damage to selected, highly visible targets in Britain ended. The campaign was largely a failure, as both British and Irish governments upped the ante and cracked down on known or suspected IRA members. With renewed determination, however, the Provisionals resumed their attacks in Northern Ireland. On 7 October, a twin-car bomb exploded inside British army headquarters in Lisburn, Co. Antrim. Only one soldier was killed, but the assault was proof the Provos could still inflict serious damage when and where they chose. The sleeping giant had reawakened.

My following reaction to the Lisburn bombing was written on 11 November 1996, the 78th anniversary of the First War's Armistice Day. It was published as a Letter to the Editor in the *Irish Echo* (New York City) ten days later.

❧

THE PIECES OF PEACE...I was distressed and discouraged flying back to the States after the Lisburn bombing. The chance for any meaningful talks between unionists and nationalists is over, at least for now. The people holding power really do not want peace! I wonder if they ever did.

It does not take an eejit to read the paint-splattered walls. How is it possible to talk peace without Sinn Fein in attendance? Though they represent only fifteen percent of the vote, they are fifty percent of the problem and its solution. The key unionists, Ian Paisley, leader of the Democratic Unionist Party, and David Trimble, head of the Ulster Unionist Party, are not willing to give up one iota of power, position or prestige. Gerry Adams, president of Sinn Fein, seems to have lost influence, if he ever had any, with the hard-line republicans. While the Protestant and Catholic man and woman in the street hungers for peace, selfish narrow-minded politicians keep the pot stirred up with everyone's fears on razor's edge.

The British government is unwilling to be decisive, America's leadership is too preoccupied with its own problems, and no one pays much attention to what the Dublin bureaucrats say.

If time allows, maybe Britain's Labour Party and the Northern Irish people themselves might have enough fortitude, after the next general election, to organise some truly meaningful discussions. With the unfolding of some creative decision-making on everyone's part, a new 'Home Rule' scheme might materialise from a combined London-Dublin-Belfast brain trust, bringing an end to British military occupation in the Six Counties. They might also be able to orchestrate meaningful, unilateral arms decommissioning that fosters the security and the freedom that all deserve.

With such a hopeful prognosis, life might just settle down, allowing for a creative, intelligent and rational Anglo-Irish, Northern Irish government to emerge. Yes, Michael (Collins), the 'stepping stones' are there...if only we have the courage to use them....

TIME TO FORGIVE & FORGET…

TIME TO FORGIVE
& FORGET...

The Irish have a hard time doing this...forgetting. So too do some American political pundits. Apparently, Cal Thomas is one of these people. In his 16 March 1995 editorial, this syndicated columnist takes a stab at both Gerry Adams, leader of Sinn Fein, the Irish political party with ties to the Irish Republican Army (IRA), and President Bill Clinton. The American leader, according to Thomas, "...overruled the advice of most of his foreign policy advisers and allowed Gerry Adams to return to the United States this week to conduct fund-raising activities for his terrorist Sinn Fein organization, which has been responsible for the deaths of innocent civilians in Britain and Northern Ireland." Mr. Thomas goes on to comment that President Clinton's decision was "a crass appeal for Irish votes in the United States."

The columnist notes that talks with the British government, IRA and Sinn Fein are in the beginning stages, and that the key issue of decommissioning IRA weapons is far from resolved. Allowing Adams to raise funds in the States is likely to be viewed as American support for "...subsidizing a continuing war against innocent people and the British government, our [America's] supposed close ally."

To his credit, Mr. Thomas mentions that the IRA has "mostly" lived up to its promised cease-fire, and that the British principle of "progressive disarmament" is still on the bargaining table, assuming it is part of an agreeable verification procedure.

Two weeks later, the essence of my rejoinder to Mr. Thomas's column, as seen below, appeared in *The Daily Progress* (Charlottesville, Virginia).

TIME TO FORGIVE & FORGET…In Mr. Cal Thomas's editorial of 16 March 1995 entitled "Honoring Sinn Fein's leader Adams, Clinton is playing a dangerous game," he condemns President Clinton's invitation to Gerry Adams and Sinn Fein to St. Patrick's Day festivities on Capitol Hill. Unfortunately, Mr. Thomas's position is very deceptive.

The Irish Republican Army (IRA) did not begin, or is it solely responsible for, the violence in Northern Ireland (NI). Discounting the historic battles between the Irish clans and Queen Elizabeth I in the sixteenth century and the Glorious Revolution fought in Ireland one hundred years later, organised violence in Ulster began with the formation of the Protestant Orange Order in 1795. Previously, the Protestant Ascendancy society, buoyed up by armed bands known as the Peep-O-Day boys, looked the other way as these gangs of vigilantes terrorised Catholic and Presbyterian Dissenters. Those unionists, loyal to the Crown, vigorously protected their political, economic and social privileges in Ulster.

In the twentieth century, acts of violence on both sides of the religious and political divide, first produced by the British government's partitioning of Ireland in 1920 and later resulting in the fight for civil rights in the late-1960s, have sadly carried on the old tradition of conflict and division. In reality, all sides in this quarrel share the blame, not just one or the other.

During the past twenty-five years, Protestant and Catholic, unionist and nationalist, loyalist and republican are responsible for an almost equal number of deaths (3,200) and terrorist incidents. It is not the one-sided affair Mr. Thomas paints. Protestant/loyalist paramilitary groups such as the LVF

(Loyalist Volunteer Force), UVF (Ulster Volunteer Force), UFF (Ulster Freedom Fighters) and UDA (Ulster Defence Association) have hidden weapons too. The IRA is not the only guilty party. Today, there seems to be little pressure to bring loyalists to the bargaining table, to decommission their illegally-held weapons, to stop their 'punishment beatings' and to account for their vast fund-raising efforts.

Unfortunately, individuals championed by the likes of Cal Thomas have the least to gain. They are afraid, as the nationalist community stands up and is counted, NI will slowly be absorbed back into the Irish Republic. The unionists fear they will eventually lose their present-day secure political, economic and social status. Consequently, their elitism will come to an end, as a truly new and democratic society evolves. By keeping the focus on the IRA, with the emphasis on its violent past, those wishing to keep northern Irish society divided are being successful. It seems it is more popular to stress dissension and division than harmony and unity.

To construct a viable peace agenda, all parties and all issues need to be brought together around the negotiating table. Britain, Ireland and the United States need to uphold the democratic rights of all groups in NI. There needs to be an end to injustice and inequality on all sides. The people of the Six Counties must be allowed to live in peace in a demilitarised and unoccupied country...be it united with the Irish Republic, a part of the United Kingdom or as a newly designed and separate entity.

It is time to forgive and forget. The United States traditionally has followed such a path. It forgave Germany, Italy, Japan, Viet Nam and is in the process of forgiving China, North Korea and member countries of the former Soviet Union. Isn't it time to pardon the Irish Republican Army as well?

Mr. Thomas must forgive and forget too! On this St. Patrick's Day, Mr. Clinton held out the olive branch to Mr. Adams and to forty-four million Irish-Americans. Besides playing the American political game of appealing to a large block of potential voters, the President also offered encouragement to one small part of this world, as it continues its yearning for peace and reconciliation.

TOWARD PEACE & UNITY IN IRELAND...

TOWARD PEACE & UNITY IN IRELAND...

The following editorial was written one week after the Good Friday Peace Accord was reached in Belfast, Northern Ireland, 10 April 1998. It was published in the May, 1998 issue of *Dream Weaver* (Cincinnati, Ohio), a magazine dedicated to featuring local Ohio, Kentucky and Indiana writers.

TOWARD PEACE & UNITY IN IRELAND...The recent Good Friday, British-Irish agreement has stirred up almost as much controversy as its 1922 predecessor.

Eighty-one years ago Ireland signed an agreement with Britain after a bitter two-year war for independence. Then, the two differing elements within the newly created twenty-six county Irish Free State, the pro- and anti-treatyites, were unable to agree among themselves over the conditions of 'the treaty.' As a consequence, they fought a divisive civil war, trying to assert their separate positions.

The fractured remains of that disagreement continue to fester today. Often referred to as 'the Troubles,' this particularly heinous residue, spawned almost a century ago, lives on in a six-county political entity known as Northern Ireland (NI). Today, unionists seek to remain under the protective umbrella of Britain while nationalists long for a united Ireland. In what may be NI's last opportunity for lasting peace in years, its people must unite and support the Good Friday Agreement.

Political infighting among the unionist majority in the North can only weaken their Victorian position and expose their militant hatefulness. In the meantime, the northern nationalist minority must pressure their republican defenders to emerge from their cocoon of military conquest and fight future engagements on the political battlefield, not in city streets. It is time for the island of Ireland to reject the age-old culture of armed conflict and seize the opportunity for understanding through peaceful means.

After all, loyalism was born to maintain the Ulster link with Britain by any design, while republicanism is dedicated to uniting Ireland through whatever means are necessary to achieve that aim. But today, this new cross-border pact offers both sides a chance to pursue their individual objectives across the conference table and at the ballot box instead of in narrow-minded alleyways and over freshly dug graves.

May all sides see the light and not let this window of hope be extinguished by the hand of selfish, myopic extremists. Please God, may a peaceful and 'united' Ireland finally seek its place, as Robert Emmet dreamed, "among the nations of the earth."

(Note: In a national referendum on 22 May 1998, the first such one since December, 1918, the people of Ireland, both north and south, overwhelmingly endorsed the Good Friday Agreement. Now, if the document's implementation were only as simple.)

EASTERTIDE &
THE IRISH...

EASTERTIDE & THE IRISH...

Eastertide & The Irish is the first of two short essays as well as a poem, all serving as introduction and background to a chapter taken from my book, *Consumed in Freedom's Flame: A Novel of Ireland's Struggle for Freedom 1916-1921,* first published in January, 2001 by St. Padraic Press (Cincinnati, Ohio).

My interest in the 1916 Easter Rebellion is long-standing. It stems from the stories I have heard, the books I have read, but most significantly, it springs from the men and women I have known who lived through those troubled times.

You see, in my mind, history is a living, evolving thing...never static, always changing. Certainly though, the evolution of history is not always a simple or easy process. Its re-examination creates controversy and disagreement along with, hopefully, evolving clarity. Sometimes facts and opinion become confused with one another. Cognitive and affective dissonance are often the by-product of historical examination.

Irish history has certainly not escaped the reviewer's pen. Happily though, it tends to produce a view of yesterday that is less insular, more reasoned and diverse. On the other hand, who is to say the revisionists are always accurate in their analysis? Sure, is political correctness always right?

Simply stated, however, I believe history, besides chronicling the past, is meant to honour the dead and to inspire the living. That is what these 1916 writings are about. They are not intended to open old wounds. Rather, they are advanced to describe a turbulent window in Irish history that has influenced its past and shaped its present. This is particularly so of Dublin's 1916 Easter Rebellion: Ireland's most dramatic and historically important watershed event of the twentieth century.

The following selections are meant to honour the men and women who sacrificed so much for Irish freedom almost a century ago. Sure, these are the heroes whose efforts deserve to be remembered and better understood.

Finally, my writings try to capture what it must have been like living in Ireland a hundred years ago or so, with the ever-present threat of the Stranger's lash lurking overhead....

This first piece was written in the spring of 1998.

EASTERTIDE & THE IRISH...As the days stretch out with the arrival of spring, both Catholics and Protestants in Ireland, each according to their own traditions, honour Christ's Passion with Paschal remembrances. These acts continue to reflect Ireland's pagan past and celebrate its Christian present.

But Eastertide in Ireland is special for another reason. Partly motivated by the symbolism inherent in Christ's resurrection, Ireland's twentieth-century Father-of-Independence, Patrick Henry Pearse, is also lovingly remembered. As Ireland's first president and military commander, Pearse led a small group of Irish revolutionaries against the might of the British Empire in April, 1916. Though brutally crushed in five short days, this brief but bloody insurrection marked the advent of Ireland's most dramatic and fateful thrust for freedom in its turbulent and often barbarous 750 years of foreign occupation.

Traditionally, Ireland's past has strongly influenced its present-day thinking. Today, however, it is more politically correct for Irish nationalists, those wishing to see Ireland's six northeastern counties brought into the Republic, to de-emphasise their stormy 1916 birthright. This is in deference to the sensitivities of their unionist neighbours, who wish for a continuance of their 1801 union with England. In contrast, however, northern unionists seem less concerned with respecting nationalists' feelings as they continue to celebrate their political origins. This genesis arises from Protestant King William III of Orange's victory over Catholic King James II's forces at the Battle of the Boyne (Co. Meath) in 1690.

The Orange Order, founded a century later, eclipsed William's traditional birthday celebration, 4 November. This fraternity substituted the Boyne-triumph, 12 July, as the centrepiece of its Protestant society. The 'marching season,' as it is called, traditionally sees hundreds of sectarian parades held throughout the Six Counties during July and August. Unfortunately, these activities continue to be a festering hotbed of hatred and violence. This blatant triumphalism is often the source of international news reporting, featuring clashes between members of these two Northern Irish communities.

Historically speaking, several dynamics collided, sparking the 1916 Easter Rebellion. The Rising itself, led by a small group of romantic and revolutionary-minded nationalists, saw Britain's European war difficulties (WWI) as their opportunity to break the hated link connecting them to England. These events had both political and cultural overtones.

For almost fifty years, Britain's parliament had failed to reach an agreeable accommodation regarding Home Rule in Ireland. This caused a great deal of friction, especially among diehard separatists like Pearse and socialist union-leader James Connolly.

From a cultural viewpoint, the turn of the twentieth century saw a rekindling of Ireland's Gaelic past, both mythical and real. There was a genuine rebirth of interest in the Irish language, the arts, history, culture and sport.

This growing fermentation was further enhanced when Ulster unionists, mainly Protestant, began flexing their military muscles in a bold attempt to remain free of a Britishproposed Dublin government, mainly controlled by Irish Catholics. A growing threat of Irish civil war or of belligerent Ulster's possible breaking away from British authority posed a serious threat to nationalist Ireland's hopes for unity.

Additionally, Ireland recently experienced a period of labour unrest and fledgling union organization. For the first time in history, urban Irish workers stood up to their grasping employers. James Larkin had sparked their demand for fair wages and humane working conditions. Moving from Belfast to Dublin, this son of poor Irish emigrants founded the Irish Transport and General Workers' Union (ITGWU) in 1909. He recruited thousands of members from Dublin's vast pool of unskilled slum dwellers. These men, long overworked, underpaid and subjected to some of the worst living conditions in Europe, soon became an economic and social force for change in Ireland.

In 1913, Dublin's foremost employers locked-out their employees, as they collectively hoped to break the union's might. After six months, the ITGWU gave in and its members were forced to return to work. As a result, out of personal necessity, Larkin left Ireland for the United States. Before doing so, however, he handed the reins of power over to James Connolly. It was this same revolutionary socialist who had organized a small army in 1913 to protect the union's membership from the vicious attacks of the Dublin Metropolitan Police. From then onward, Connolly, his Irish Citizen Army and his inherited labour party began playing a important role in Ireland's drive for self-government.

This very pithy look into early twentieth-century Irish dynamics exposes some of the convergent forces precipitating the violent 1916 eruption. This conflict would later become the source of much of present-day Ireland's political difficulties.

On the one hand, independence for twenty-six of its thirty-two counties sprang to life in 1922: a direct result of the

Easter Rebellion. Sadly, however, it set into motion the political machinery that led to the island's partitioning in 1920.

Today, poised on the brink of a new understanding, Dublin, Belfast, London and Washington still wrestle with the political antagonisms resulting from that vernal struggle. England's first colony, Ireland, is slowly marching down the road to being her last, though she is not quite there yet. In the final analysis, the world can only speculate that were it not for the courage and vision of the men and women of '16, there might not be any Irish Republic today, as imperfect as it may be.

EASTER, 1916
REMEMBERED...

EASTER, 1916 REMEMBERED...

This tribute was re-penned in February, 2002.

EASTER, 1916 REMEMBERED...As the 86th anniversary of the 1916 Easter Rebellion draws nigh, let us look back at that watershed moment in Irish history of which William Butler Yeats wrote, "All changed, changed utterly..." and of the Rising's leadership who gave their lives so Ireland might one day be free.

...and we pause to remember their names...Thomas Clarke, Eamonn Ceannt and Sean MacDiarmada....

It is not possible to isolate one specific incident and pinpoint it as the cause that sparked the Rebellion of '16. Rather than a solitary event, Ireland witnessed the collision of numerous dynamic forces. Dramatically, they all coalesced during a narrow window of time, precipitating Dublin's violent eruption. Even today, almost a century later, Ireland and Great Britain are still dealing with its momentous repercussions.

On the surface, it would be accurate to say that the Rising occurred because the Supreme Council of the Irish Republican Brotherhood (IRB) decided to stage a revolt. In due course, it was this small group of romantic, revolutionary nationalists who chose to follow in their Fenian-forefathers' physical-force footsteps. So clandestinely, in the autumn of 1914, the IRB decided that Britain's war difficulties in Europe was their opportunity 'to break the hated connexion with England.' It was a tether that had bound the two islands together for over seven hundred and fifty years. Resolutely but warily, they began beating their drum of war.

The IRB's need for secrecy was paramount. Ireland's past was sadly pockmarked with stories of informers destroying the carefully laid plans of other disaffected revolutionaries. Now it was their turn, their generation's chance to rise up for the cause of liberty. It was an opportunity they vowed not to miss.

Despite their impatience, the Brotherhood's military decision to act was only one part of the story. In addition to their revolutionary determination, other influences were colliding beyond the Brotherhood's control. Together, these forces would help slake their thirsty patriotic palates.

...and we pause to remember their names...Joseph Mary Plunkett, Thomas MacDonagh and Sean Heuston....

One of those dynamics, be it a blessing or a curse, radiated from Ireland's perpetual obsession with evoking memories of its troubled past. This haunting coloured its political evolution, clearly influencing the leading decision makers of the day. Nineteenth and early twentieth-century constitutional nationalists such as Daniel O'Connell, Isaac Butt, Charles Stewart Parnell, John Redmond and Arthur Griffith used Henry Grattan's late eighteenth-century Irish Parliament, its 1782 constitution and its Protestant patriot movement as springboards for their own political agendas. Furthermore, the general resurgence of European nationalism coupled with the often unwelcome tradition of Britain's centuries-old domination of its island neighbour continually fuelled the growing fire.

As the nineteenth century came to a close, a third pressure emerged in the appearance of a renewed interest in the rebirth of an Irish Ireland. Drawing strength from Eireann's Gaelic past, cultural revivalists focused attention on Ireland's suppressed and forgotten tongue. They revelled in the rebirth of Irish language, literature, sport, music, art and other ancient cultural appendages. This reverence for the past was spurred on by the burning desire to rekindle Ireland's days of past glory: be they real or imagined.

A fourth force plying its influence on 1916 Ireland orbited about the political struggles designed to effect some form of Home Rule legislation that would satisfy both Irish nationalist and unionist. Finally, in the summer of 1914, after years of debate and compromise, an act allowing Ireland to manage much of its own domestic affairs passed muster in Westminster. Its immediate implementation, however, was placed on hold until the war in Europe was won. Most Irish Catholics, being constitutional nationalists at heart, seemed satisfied with the agreement, but a small core of hardened republicans was not. Their intent was out-and-out independence, not partial subservience.

Besides the divisive influence mentioned above, other forces were at work. The discordant demands of Ireland's Ulster unionists, seeking to remain free of a Dublin, Home-Ruled 'Popish' parliament let their displeasures be known. These northerners wanted to remain within the Union. If forced, however, to be a part of a 'united Ireland,' they were ready to belligerently establish their own provisional government. Prepared to declare their independence from Britain and boldly fight to defend 'their' Ulster, these quasi-militant secessionists were advocating sedition and civil war. They were supported by a solemn covenant signed by one-third of Ulster's population, were backed by a military force of 100,000 rifled men and were led by a strident leader, Edward Carson, who pledged, "Ulster will fight and Ulster will be right."

...and we pause to remember their names...William Pearse, Michael Mallin and Edward Daly....

Still more trouble was afoot. The steady Anglicisation of Irish society alarmed some perceptive political pundits. Following the 1801 Act of Union, Britain granted Irish Catholics emancipation. Then, on the heels of the tragedies surrounding the famine of Black '47, Ireland's sorrow and England's shame, Westminster showed a heightened sensitivity toward its neighbour to the west. As a concession to Ireland's Catholic citizenry, Britain passed legislation disestablishing and disendowing all Church of Ireland obligations. Next, a London-Dublin government approved acts reforming land ownership, establishing local county councils and gradually eliminating the hated institution of the Anglo-Irish landlord. Some, however, feared the handwriting on the wall. They detested perfidious Albion's continued insidious controlling influence at all levels of Irish affairs. The objectionists reasoned, "What Britannia gives us now may be taken away later, for isn't our past scarred with her broken promises?"

The growing revolutionary pressures of physical-force intervention, Irish nationalism, cultural revivalism, Home Rule opposition, Ulster's blatant defiance and Ireland's encroaching Anglicisation approached critical mass in the years leading up to 1916.

Finally, with the formal organisation and arming of Ulster by its determined leadership, the nationalists had a legitimate excuse to establish a military presence of their own. Though not as well armed or as highly motivated as its northern countrymen, the south of Ireland formed its own voluntary body in late 1913. Its stated purpose was to protect Eireann's shores from foreign invasion, to oppose London's forced conscription of Irishmen into the British Army and to ensure, by force if necessary, the timely implementation of Home Rule after the First World War had ended. Rebel anti-British subversives, however, saw this newly formed volunteer corps as providing the necessary backbone Ireland needed to support its drive for a full measure of national independence. Stealthily, the IRB infiltrated the Irish Volunteer organisation.

Final plans gradually coalesced. They culminated in a call to arms on Easter Monday, 24 April 1916. On that day, Ireland witnessed the dawning of a 'terrible beauty.' The Easter Rebellion had begun.

...and we pause to remember their names...Michael O'Hanrahan, Con Colbert and John MacBride....

History clearly records what befell Dublin's Eastertide rebels. The forces of the Crown won out in the short term, but six years later surrendered most of their power and influence to the newly formed Irish Free State government.

Sadly, however, the island of Ireland continues to grapple with the legacies of Easter Week. On the one hand, independence for twenty-six of its thirty-two counties sprang to life. On the other, the Rebellion set into motion the political machinery leading to Ireland's partitioning in 1920. It also led to a bitter civil war when its citizens could not agree on how to ratify the treaty negotiated by their new government in 1922. Regrettably, it is the residue of these heavy burdens that Ireland, England, America and the world still wrestle with today.

...and we pause to remember their names...Thomas Kent, Roger Casement, James Connolly and Patrick Henry Pearse....

THE IRISH REBEL...

THE IRISH REBEL...

Originally entitled "Murder," the following selection is a short chapter taken from my novel entitled *Consumed in Freedom's Flame: A Novel of Ireland's Struggle for Freedom* 1916-1921. Published in 2001 by St. Padraic Press (Cincinnati, Ohio), this work weaves historical fact and fiction around the events surrounding the 1916 Easter Rebellion and Ireland's War of Independence, 1919-1921.

The book is the story of a fictional hero, Aran Roe O'Neill, and his resolute commitment to Ireland and its quest for independence. Aran and his friends, both factual and fictional, personify the courageous resistance of generations of Irishmen and women to English conquest, corruption and injustice.

Aran, the Irish Rebel, is a seventeen-year-old young man, the son of a farmer from Gort in Co. Galway. This youthful hero becomes caught up in the excitement, the danger and the tragedy of Ireland s rush toward independence and self-government. In my mind, Aran embodies what the ordinary man or woman, living in Ireland during the early part of the twentieth century, might have done, if they too had shared some of his thoughts, feelings and determination. What was it about this mythical dream that drove so many Irish citizens to risk life, limb and property for the cause of liberty? My fictionalized character grapples with that question and its answer.

In the following selection, Aran has managed to escape the British dragnet thrown up around Dublin after the collapse of the Easter Rebellion. With nowhere else to go, he heads for the safety of the Wicklow Mountains before beginning his long walk home. It is there, on an isolated mountainside above Glendalough, that he finds shelter in a small animal shed. During the night, as a terrible storm rages through the mountains, Aran has a frightening dream. It is about his friend, teacher and leader of the failed Rebellion, Patrick Henry Pearse. Several more days will pass, however, before the Irish Rebel fully understands the meaning of his distressing nightmare. This is the story of that night and Aran's dream.

If you enjoy this tidbit from the book, I hope you will read the entire story of Aran s adventures. The volume's sequel, *Blood On The Shamrock: A Novel of Ireland's Continued Struggle for Freedom 1921-1924* will be in bookstores in mid-2004.)

THE IRISH REBEL...The late afternoon turned soft. Aran Roe pulled the collar of Thomas's jacket up around his neck in a vain attempt to keep the gentle spring rain from soaking him through to the skin. Walking over the rough, uneven ground of the Wicklows, Aran wished he had his old broad, black brimmer to shelter him. Like his father, he believed if your head was protected from the weather, the rain and damp were not so bad.

Alone, the young Irish Rebel trod on through the drizzly gathering gloom. As he went, he thought back over the events of the morning. He had been on his feet with only one short break since yesterday evening. More than eighteen hours had passed since he had eaten or rested properly. Hunger and fatigue were now his only companions and, though he felt tired and off colour, Aran knew it was vitally important for him to keep moving west through the mountains and away from Roundwood.

Ignoring the mighty weariness slowly enveloping him, the Gortman doggedly maintained his measured stride and steady forward progress. He was proud of his recent accomplishments but wise enough not to take any foolish chances at this late date. Despite his fatigue, his senses were on full alert.

He actively refused to let the intoxicating power of the Rebellion's residue go to his head...especially after all he had been through to come this far.

Outwardly, the cut of him would have turned many a head. An odd collection of borrowed, dirt-stained clothing girded his six-foot frame, cloaking his muscular physique. Aran's once shiny black boots now were covered with mud. His hands were filthy while his thick, curly-brown, unkempt hair looked oily and matted from the day's damp.

Inwardly, Aran was not his usual self either. As the day wore on, his energy reserves neared the point of exhaustion. He was tired, hungry and felt out of sorts. Despite all this, however, his coal-black eyes still sparkled, fired by some deep well of inner strength. His unusually taut facial expression now seldom revealed the youthful playfulness born of happier and more innocent times.

On he slogged with slowing pace as night began to close in around him. Calling upon his dwindling stores, the young man skirted north around the beautiful valley of Glendalough, famous for its Saints both Kevin and Lawrence O'Toole. With heightened concentration, he pressed on through open fields and along winding trails compacted by generations of meandering sheep. All around him low hanging clouds clung to the mountaintops while a rising mist issued forth from the glen below. Occasionally, a wintry-like rain shower peppered down on him from an increasingly foreboding sky. A bad situation was rapidly becoming worse.

The fear, however, from what he fled was overpowering. He did not have to remind himself how important it was to keep moving westward. So, staying above the sparse tree line, the Irish Rebel made his way across country over marginal pasture land. His path was often criss-crossed with clumps of heather, patches of grass sprinkled with stands of yellow furze all accented by frequent outcroppings of rocky granite. There were few houses or people living in this part of the Wicklow

Mountains. This grassy boggy land was used almost exclusively for cattle and sheep grazing by local farmers.

In this remote part of the Irish countryside there was only a solitary road heading west through the mountains. From Aran's vantage point just below the ridge line, the retreating soldier had an excellent view of its winding path. If they were still on his trail, the fleeing Irishman knew the British military or Royal Irish Constabulary would have a difficult time surprising him up there.

To the Gortman, raised on the west coast of Ireland, those two groups were the embodiment of economic oppression and political domination. The British for so long had one hand in Ireland's pocket and the other around its throat. Aran had been reminded of this fact over and over while growing up in a household strongly governed by its nationalistic sentiments. Aided by a sound formal education and accelerated by his early maturity, Aran was outraged and incensed at the Saxon Stranger's seven-hundred-year-plus dominance of his homeland. He knew of Eireann's long suffering and, with a deepening sense of loathing and disgust for British politics, this youth had vowed to do something about standing up for Irish independence. That and self-preservation were the main reasons for his now rigorous march through the Wicklows in less than desirable circumstances.

Though on his own this dirty evening, Aran Roe was well armed and, hopefully, prepared for most eventualities. He had one revolver tucked in his belt under his jacket, another concealed in the haversack slung over his right shoulder and a single-barreled shotgun bobbed up and down in the crook of his left arm.

Prior to fleeing the barracks in Roundwood, Aran had selected a shotgun instead of a rifle for protection. He thought its presence would attract less attention in the countryside than a military-like rifle. Besides, it would support his carefully concocted cover story of being on an Easter holiday hunting excursion from his Dublin suburban school.

He trudged on. In an effort to ward off the hellish effects of numbing fatigue, Aran recalled the myriad stories that had circulated throughout Dublin Town after the IRA's unconditional surrender. These rumours vowed that the ringleaders would be dealt with in 'a most severe manner.' As President and Commander-in-Chief of the newly declared Irish Republic, Pearse's life might be forfeited. But, what about the others? Would the British execute them all?

For the past several months, Aran had listened to his beloved Pearse speculate about his death in battle or, if the Rebellion should fail, his execution by the aggrieved English. Neither eventuality seemed to trouble this romantic intellectual. No, Pearse was not afraid to die for his country. This thoughtful educator firmly believed that the Irish people must be awakened from their slumber and given a new sense of hope, thus sparking a renewed desire for freedom from their present colonial overlords.

Pearse maintained that every Irish generation had the responsibility to rise up and demand its independence. Once he even told Aran that he believed bloodshed was a cleansing and sanctifying thing and that any nation who regarded it as its final horror had lost its manhood.

The schoolteacher believed that those who died fighting for Ireland's cause gave their lives so this ancient land could be reborn. Aran remembered Pearse's hero, Robert Emmet. He had died a brutal death at the hands of the Sassenach after his aborted 1803 Rebellion. Pearse said Emmet died for Ireland so Eireann might once again be free.

No, Pearse was not afraid of death. His Ireland was a cause worth living, fighting and dying for. Those close to him knew and understood that his Irish passions ran deep.

Aran thought of the people with whom he had brushed

shoulders during the past week and of his St. Enda's class-
mates. What was going to happen to the school now? Would
the British destroy it for its symbolic representation of Pearse's
defiance of their power and authority? What of Pearse's mother?
His two sisters? Would the Stranger arrest them or worse?
What of Pearse's brother Willie? He never really played an
active role in the planning or fighting. He was just Patrick's
friend and brotherly sounding board.

Aran recalled the night he had spent as a prisoner in Richmond Barracks. His brief exchanges with Michael Collins
had a powerful impact on him. Collins shared the same fierce
drive for freedom from England that both Pearse and he felt.
The Corkman, however, expressed his feelings more directly
and with less poetic idealism than did Aran's beloved teacher.
Hopefully, the three of them would survive all this and continue, somehow, fighting for their native land's independence.

Aran realised that Easter 1916 had been Pearse's turn...his
generation's opportunity to strike for freedom. They had all
fought well...even to the bitter end. But now it might be up
to himself and others to carry on the age-old struggle.

Now, with heavy black rain clouds overhead, darkness
quickly closed in around Aran Roe O'Neill. If only he had a
home-cooked meal and a warm bed waiting for him just over
the next rise, but that was too much to wish for up here in the
mountains. Then, Aran smiled to himself. Wasn't he the seventh son of a seventh son? His father and grandfather had
often told him of a special aura that encompassed him. It was
there for his protection and safekeeping. They had often talked
in hushed tones about this unique force and unusual dividend that was part of his birthright. Suddenly shivering with
cold, Aran quickly reflected over the events of the last ten

days. He wondered if there might not be some truth in their superstitious beliefs after all.

As the immediacy of night bore down upon him, the young rebel's thoughts turned to a more practical issue when he spied a small shed up ahead. With no prospects of anything better to serve as shelter, he headed up a steep slope covered with lush green grass dotted with little patches of yellow buttercups.

To his delight the shed was empty and even some clean, dry straw was piled in one corner. He carefully spread it on the floor opposite the door thinking to himself that if anyone should happen to barge in on him tonight, they would have a rude awakening looking down the barrel of his loaded shotgun.

Not daring to light a small fire for fear of attracting unwanted company, Aran sat down and leaned back against the shed's wall. The tiny structure was bathed in silent darkness. Slowly, he ate the last remaining bits of food left in his haversack. It was neither filling nor tasty and did not satisfy his peckishness.

After finishing his solitary meal, Aran curled up on his bed of straw. He was slowly drying off, but his still-damp clothes clung to his skin, making falling asleep difficult.

Before succumbing to his fatigue the Gortman recollected some of the stories Major John McBride had told him of living rough when he had fought with the Boer guerrillas in the Transvaal during the 1899-1902 Boer War. It was a new kind of war that used hit-and-run tactics instead of conventional military assaults. McBride had helped organise an Irish Brigade to fight the British back in those days. He had sided with the Dutch farmers in their quest for independence. Later, in 1910, that land was annexed and became part of the new Union of South Africa. But before its political amalgamation, the English had staked their claim to the newly discovered

South African gold fields and diamond mines. Again, British imperial greed would stop at nothing short of total victory as their ever-expanding colonial lust cried out for more.

In addition to both sides refining the art of guerrilla warfare at the turn of the century, British Major General Horatio Herbert Kitchener, born 1850 in Ballylongford, County Kerry, Ireland, introduced the world to another new first, the concentration camp. In his now infamous 'relocation camps,' thousands of Boer women, children and old men died of disease, malnutrition and abuse. Always willing to overlook their own faults for their own greater good, the appreciative English venerated Kitchener for bringing the war to a successful British conclusion.

Today, this fabled warrior was serving as Great Britain's Secretary of State for War. His latest brainchild saw men from the same family as well as those from neighbouring villages and towns all assigned to the same battalions fighting in France. These Kitchener 'buddy units' were intended to raise the men's morale and sharpen their fighting spirit. It may have accomplished those ends, but as the war dragged on, those special units of British soldiers were forced to charge from their trenches across the muddy killing-fields of France. Britain's battle-weary frustrations were urged on by their foolhardy desire to bring the war to a rapid end. Their misguided battlefield tactics resulted in tragedy, not victory.

Those fields of war, clogged with tangled barriers of razor-sharp barbed wire, swept with murderous machine gun fire and obscured by clouds of poisonous gas, witnessed the systematic decimation of British families and the masculine depopulation of entire English towns. Great Britain lost most of a generation of young men in one tragic and needless stroke of thoughtless planning and senseless annihilation.

When at last he drifted off, Aran slept fitfully. A storm raged throughout the Wicklow Mountains that night. Finally, just as dawn arrived, a tremendous flash of lightning illuminated the darkness, startling him awake. Its following clap of explosive thunder frightened him so that he sat bolt upright clutching his shotgun.

It took Aran several seconds to regain control of his panicked emotions. Cautiously, he pulled himself up onto his feet, opened the shelter's door and peered out. The rain had stopped and the storm had vanished. Morning's faint glow etched itself into the eastern sky as Aran's eyes searched the waning darkness for any signs of movement.

Finally, with his heart still pounding but satisfied he was alone, he returned to his straw pallet. The brilliant flash of lightning and its accompanying crack of thunder had marked the end of the night's storm.

Two days were to pass before Aran learned that at dawn, on the third of May, the day of the RIC barracks' raid and the night of the big storm, Patrick Henry Pearse, the first President of the Irish Republic, was executed by a British firing squad in Stonebreaker's Yard, Kilmainham Gaol, Dublin.

Over time, Aran pieced together the events surrounding his teacher's death. After Pearse's surrender to General Lowe and his son on Saturday afternoon, the 29th, the English drove Pearse to Parkgate, British Military Headquarters, to meet with Ireland's new British Commander-in-Chief, General Sir John Grenfell Maxwell. There was little to discuss, however, as Pearse had unconditionally surrendered.

Besides a personal fascination for meeting his defeated foe face to face, Maxwell, an ardent believer in the Empire, wanted Pearse to dictate the Order to Surrender instructions to his four Dublin battalion commanders. Aran found it interesting that Connolly's Second-In-Command and Chief of Staff, Michael Mallin, refused to obey Pearse's surrender orders until Connolly, his Commandant, had added his personal instructions and signature to those of Pearse.

By Sunday evening, all rebel positions had been reoccupied by the British authorities and all the freedom-fighters, except those lucky enough to escape, were under military arrest.

Later on that Saturday evening, Patrick Pearse was driven to Arbour Hill Barracks and placed in solitary confinement. He remained so imprisoned until Tuesday morning, May 2nd, when he was transferred to Richmond Barracks for court-martial and sentencing. Additionally, Tom Clarke and Tom MacDonagh were tried, convicted and sentenced that same day.

The English Field-General Courts-Martial were directed by British General Charles Blackadder and three other associates. These four men were British through and through.

Like so many of their judicial predecessors, they possessed no interest or knowledge about the centuries of Anglo-Irish conflicts including its social-religious persecutions or its political-economic intrigues. Their understanding of the relationship between the two island neighbours was nil. Unfortunately, this historical void prevented the magistrates from forming an opinion founded on a factual, realistic and fair-minded point of view. Their bias, strictly speaking, was British, British, British. The court's foundation was an imperial one born of colonial domination, suppression and submission to the British Crown, the British parliament and the British army.

In addition to its one-sidedness, proper legal proceedings were not followed. Though courteous to the Irish revolutionary leaders, they denied the prisoners their right of counsel. Additionally, they were refused their right to cross-examine witnesses for the prosecution while some were not permitted to call witnesses in their behalf. The court did allow the rebel leaders one concession. In front of the assembled judges and prior to sentencing, the prisoners were permitted to make a statement in defence of their actions and to offer justification for their 'offensive and illegal actions.' In the true spirit of Robert Emmet, some took the opportunity to utter inspired and thoughtful declarations while others offered simple statements in defence of their beliefs, motives and character.

As a fitting and final touch, no court stenographer was permitted to be present, so the trial dialogue was recorded in longhand. This greatly slowed the proceedings. Later, this omission prevented an accurate review of the trial's sequence of events and its sworn testimonies.

In reality, all the courts-martial trials were nothing more than kangaroo courts orchestrated and controlled by General Maxwell and his lieutenants. Though the British did try to give the hearings the appearance of proper legal deportment, they were simply and carefully covering their own tracks as they prepared to carry out the most heinous of deeds.

When their trials were ended and their death sentences pronounced, Pearse, Clarke and MacDonagh were driven from Richmond Barracks to Kilmainham Gaol. There they spent their final few hours of life united in spirit but separated by the cold stone walls of that 1796 prison.

On that same May 2nd evening, several miles from Kilmainham's bleakness, General Blackadder, surrounded by the elegance of Georgian architecture, French wine and soft candlelight, was the guest of honour at an elegant party. During dinner the conversation turned to the Rebellion and how the first day of courts-martial trials had gone. The General was said to have given some innocuous reply. When pressed further about his personal opinion of Patrick Henry Pearse, Blackadder was reported to have said, "Today, I had the most distasteful duty of sentencing to death one of the finest men I've ever had the pleasure of meeting."

One of the dinner party invitees, who secretly sympathised with the rebels' attempts at freedom, wondered if the General truly meant what he had said about Pearse or was just trying to soothe his own guilty conscience.

Patrick Henry Pearse, the uprising's figurehead, chose to pass most of his last remaining hours doing what he loved, writing. Besides recording the carefully chosen words he had spoken at his court-martial, in defence of his Easter Week actions, he wrote a short poem entitled The Wayfarer plus individual letters to his mother, sister Margaret and brother Willie.

Then, just before midnight, Pearse requested to see a priest. Father Aloysius, a Capuchin, came and gave Ireland's first president Holy Communion. It was to this man that he entrusted his last precious written thoughts.

Patrick's mother was finally given permission to visit her son. She had planned to arrive early in the morning of May 3rd. Unfortunately, the British solder sent to collect Mrs. Pearse at St. Enda's was unable to complete his assignment. Continual sporadic rebel sniper-fire made Dublin street travel too dangerous. To further compound English ineptitude, the authorities agreed, too late, to allow Willie a final visit with his brother. As he was being taken to Kilmainham, Willie and his guards heard the shots ring out that sent his brother, Pat, to his death.

Tom Clarke, the first to sign the Proclamation out of deference to his age, his loyal devotion to the cause of Irish freedom and his dedicated IRB leadership, was the first to die at dawn in that small cobblestoned courtyard on the third day of May, 1916.

MacDonagh was shot next, and, then, it was Pearse's turn. As the clock neared half three in the morning, the condemned military leader heard the soldiers marching along the prison's dank corridors. They were coming to escort him to his death. But, before Pearse left his place of confinement, the British captain in charge permitted him a final favour. Dropping to his knees one last time, the brave teacher asked God's blessing saying, "Lord, it's over! It's finished. I gladly give myself up to you and to Eireann. Please forgive me for any unjustness I've done while thirsting for righteousness."

Rising to his feet, Pearse turned to leave his solitary cell. Its opening, however, was so low that he had to stoop down to exit. As he lowered his head to leave, Pearse reminded the guards that his act of bending down was not to be interpreted as yielding to English authority or bowing to British justice.

As he walked along the dim hallway, lit only by gas-lamps, Pearse passed the cells where his two imprisoned comrades and fellow freedom fighters had dwelled. He recalled the names of other great Irish revolutionaries who too had been incarcerated in Kilmainham Gaol. Dubliner James Napper Tandy, the United Irishmen leader, who rose and fought the British in 1798, had been here. John O'Leary, O'Donovan Rossa and John Devoy, all Fenians and part of the IRB's early history begun in 1858, had walked these halls. Charles Stewart Parnell, the Irish parliamentarian and political revolutionary, had resided rather comfortably in his 'grand' cell. That was back in 1881-82 while the 'Uncrowned King of Ireland' and British Prime Minister William Gladstone bargained about rents and land control. Yes, Parnell had slept behind these same stone walls as well. But unlike Pearse and his followers, all of these earlier heroes had walked out of Kilmainham. They had lived to fight another day for Irish freedom and English justice.

Not surprisingly, Pearse thought of his great hero, Robert Emmet. It was from this prison on the twentieth of September, 1803, that the English took Emmet to his brutal execution in Thomas Street. It was said by those who were there that day that Emmet smiled as he faced death.

Now, it was his turn. He too would smile. Yes, and he also hoped that in the days and years to come the name of Patrick Henry Pearse would live in remembered glory in the hearts and minds of Irishmen and women everywhere.

At the end of the corridor, Pearse turned right and walked down the stairs. Stopped on the flagstone landing, one of his guards securely tied Pearse's hands behind his back. A blindfold was placed over his eyes and a small white patch of cloth was pinned to his jacket just over his heart.

As Pearse quietly waited with his guards in the courtyard doorway, another volley of shots echoed through the ancient prison. Thomas MacDonagh fell dead on the cobbles.

Finally, the soldiers directed the condemned president forward into the fresh early morning air heavy with the sweetness of the previous night's rain yet bitter with the bouquet of Irish blood and British gunpowder.

As Pearse walked out, he felt his way along the uneven surface of the prison yard with the soles of his boots. Reaching the far end of the cobblestoned yard, the procession stopped. His guards faced Pearse about.

Behind him and to the right of this proud revolutionary were high walls. To his left was the massive stone prison building itself. In front knelt six uniformed British soldiers. Six more stood directly behind them forming a second row of executioners...all with rifles...all ready to speed him on his way.

Early on Friday morning, the twelfth of May, Dublin Brigade Commandant James Connolly was brought to the same Kilmainham slaughter house. He was delivered by ambulance and strapped into a chair by some of the same soldiers who had faced Patrick Pearse ten days earlier. Unlike Ireland's president, however, this bold Irishman, radical socialist and confirmed rebel was unable to stand on his own. His infected left leg would not support his poisoned, dying body.

Connolly was twice wounded on Easter Thursday. On that fateful afternoon, Connolly had planned to supervise the building of a barricade on a side street near the GPO. As he left the GHQ with his men, he was grazed in the arm by a stray enemy bullet. This incident, unnoticed by his men, necessitated his immediate return to the GPO. Connolly, with the wound dressed and with his jacket sleeve hiding his bandages, came back to supervise the barricade construction. Thirty minutes later, as he returned to headquarters, Connolly was hit several times in the left ankle by sniper bullets. While bleeding and in great pain, he managed to crawl back into the safety of the General Post Office.

After the rebel leadership's surrender on Saturday afternoon, the British, fearing Connolly might die of his wounds before they could execute him, rushed him to Dublin Castle's small hospital for medical treatment.

In spite of the best care available, Connolly's condition worsened. So, thirteen days later and in violation of all known rules of military protocol regarding the treatment of wounded officers, General Maxwell's men rushed the socialist and union leader from his hospital bed to his death in Stonebreaker's Yard.

Ever the courageous soldier and brave Irishman, James Connolly urged his murderers on by crying out, "Yes, Sir, I'll pray for all brave men who do their duty according to their lights. Then he shouted, "Fire and don't make a mess of it!" Thus, James Connolly added his own blood to the growing stain that was slowly blotting out England's colonial honour and reputation as a democratic, humane and responsible world power.

Standing tall before his firing squad, President Pearse smiled as he thought Emmet might have smiled on his execution day. A great calm passed over him as he realised how few men have the opportunity to live out their dreams and how even fewer have the chance to die as they wish. He was dying for Ireland so his ancient land might again live and be free. Satisfied that his work on earth was finished and, with nothing more to be said or done, Pearse knew his wheel of life had run down.

"READY?...FIRE!"...and at that moment, Patrick Henry Pearse, Aran's beloved mentor and Ireland's first president, slipped into the arms of God and immortality...his earthly life ended.

The rainstorm's dramatic departure had frightened Aran. Lying on his bed of straw, the Irish Rebel felt a strange and terrible sense of despair well up within him. The sensation flooded his entire being. It intensified and quite overwhelmed him. Sprawled paralysed and helpless, he listened to the ringing sounds of silence.

Unable to understand his sudden anguish, Aran closed his eyes, wishing for the comfort of his family and home. With his body curled into a protective ball, the Irish Rebel gratefully fell into a deep dreamless sleep.

When he awoke two hours later, the sun shone down on him through the shed's dirt-streaked window. The unexplained terror inside him had disappeared. He felt like himself again.

Suddenly, realising the hour's lateness and that he must be off, Aran gathered up his belongings, headed out the door and, again, set off for home. 'Twas a grand morning and he had a long road to travel.

With a fine day before him, the sun's warmth on his face and a following breeze, Aran confidently resumed his westward trek. He was unaware, however, that once again the torch of Irish freedom had been passed to yet another generation...for each new beginning starts with an end.

EASTER, 1916…

EASTER, 1916...

A portion of this poem, written in the mid-1990s, was included in my book *Consumed in Freedom's Flame: A Novel of Ireland's Struggle for Freedom 1916-1921* published in January, 2001.

In the novel, Aran Roe O'Neill, the book's hero, passes by a shop in the town of Kilkenny, some days after Dublin's 1916 Easter Rebellion has collapsed. He is surprised to see pictures of Patrick Henry Pearse, the Rebellion's leader, and other Rising organisers displayed in its window.

> The photos were surrounded by bits of black cloth or paper. Hand-lettered inscriptions adorned the snaps. Several of the captions stated, 'God Save Ireland and Its Heroes!' and 'They Fought and Died So Ireland Might Be Free.'
>
> Posted in another window was a ballad sheet entitled *Easter, 1916*. Aran read the 'come-all-ye' to himself.
>
> The bottom portion of the ballad sheet had been folded over. Aran was unable to read the remainder of the tribute but it did not matter. The author of those words understood what Pearse and the rest of the IRB (Irish Republican Brotherhood) had tried to accomplish.

The following is the full text of that tribute.

EASTER, 1916...

In Saint Enda's school there gathered a group of men so
fine,
Who talked and dreamt of Ireland's freedom unknown
in their lifetime.
For Britannia had decided long ago to claim their land,
To tax and force the Irish to enrich her royal hand.
Thus with the start of World War I, a brotherhood did
plan,
That soon an Irish Rising would be heard throughout
the land.
While England was now fighting so 'small nations might
be free,'
Eireann's freedom fighters hoped to raise their harp of
liberty.

And so on Easter Monday morning, a band of men
marched out,
They declared a free Republic about which there was no
doubt.
Some people laughed, some cried, "No!" while others
paused to see,
Would dear old England finally allow little Ireland to be
free?
But soon the Sassenach did arrive with their guns and
bayonets,
To let the bloody Irish know who ruled lest some of
them forget.
As bombs did fly and bullets rained, proud Dublin
shook with fear,
But when the rebels felt death's bite, they all loudly
raised a cheer.

Again a sacrifice of blood was asked so Ireland might be
  free...
To break the bonds that held her fast in hated slavery.
On Mount Street Bridge her men did vow, "No one
  shall pass our way!"
And many a foreign soldier-boy did lie with death that
  day.
For along the River Liffey in bastions north and south,
All withstood the siege as death did pour from out the
  lion's mouth.
Six days did pass but all was lost, so Connolly, Pearse
  and Clarke,
Surrendered to the British Crown, yet freedom's fire was
  sparked.

Though Maxwell's pit of lime did wait for those who led
  the cause,
Their deeds and dreams and spoken words did give the
  people pause.
So from the Rising's muffled hopes more patriots con-
  trived a scheme,
They wanted Eireann free at last for it was her ancient
  dream.
And it did pass as time rolled by that Ireland rose once
  more,
For not even the ruthless Black and Tans could close
  dear freedom's door.
And when at last this emerald gem did gain its 'freedom
  to be free,'
'Twas only five years after Pearse marched out with his
  brave comrade Connolly.

GOD BLESS YOU,
FATHER GRIFFIN...

GOD BLESS YOU,
FATHER GRIFFIN...

This tribute to Father Griffin appeared in the 13 November 1997 issue of the *Galway Advertiser* under the headline, "Remembering Fr Griffin...murdered this week 77 years." It summarises the terrible events surrounding his death over three-quarters of a century ago and honours this brave disciple of God who gave his life for Irish freedom.

Father Griffin was not the only priest to die for Ireland during the War of Independence. Father James O'Callaghan of Clogheen and Canon Magnier of Dunmanway, both of Co. Cork, were also murdered by British forces in 1920.

GOD BLESS YOU, FATHER GRIFFIN... As we hurry through life, it is often good and fitting to pause, reflect and remember the yesterdays we have left behind. With that thought in mind, I recently walked over the Wolfe Tone Bridge, past the Claddagh Basin and into the West. As my feet carried me along Father Griffin Road toward the Crescent and Taylor's Hill, I remembered Galway's much-loved priest of generations ago. As the gathering winter's twilight closed in around me, I thought back to another Sunday night seventy-seven years ago, the night Father Michael Griffin was kidnapped, murdered and his body unceremoniously dumped into a bog above Barna village.

In 1920, Ireland was wrestling Britain for its freedom, and Father Griffin, a young curate from Rahoon Parish, Galway City, was one more tragic victim of that mighty struggle. Born in Gurteen, Co. Galway, in 1892, Michael attended secondary school in Ballinasloe and was graduated from Maynooth College and Seminary in 1917. His first assignment was as parish priest in Ennistymon, Co. Clare. A year later, in June of 1918, he was transferred to Rahoon, where he began playing an important role in the educational and religious life of the parish.

During his spare moments over the next two years, Father Griffin studied Irish, joined the Gaelic League and, as an Irish nationalist at heart, quietly supported the newly launched Sinn Fein political party.

In 1920, as Ireland's fight for independence intensified, many Catholic priests were subjected to insults, beatings and arrest, particularly at the hands of the notorious 'Black and Tans' and Auxiliary Cadets. Hundreds of other Irish sympathisers faced similar treatment.

Things in Galway reached crisis proportion in October 1920, as Michael Walsh, an urban councillor, was shot and his body dumped into the sea off Eyre's Long Walk. Father Griffin was called to administer the last rites to the dying man.

Some witnesses said that Walsh whispered the name of his murderer into the ear of the young priest. Whatever the truth was, from that day onward, rumours circulated that this young clergyman was a marked man.

Things finally came to an awful climax on Sunday evening, 14 November. After retiring for the night in his curate's presbytery at #2 Montpellier Terrace, near the Crescent, Fr. Griffin awoke to a loud knocking. After answering the door, a few hushed words were spoken. The unsuspecting priest then returned to his room, quickly dressed and quietly disappeared into the night, accompanied by several men.

Over the next few days, news of Father Griffin's abduction spread throughout Galway. Search parties were organised. Statements were issued and the matter was even raised in the British House of Commons. Some false sightings were reported.

Finally, on Saturday afternoon, November 20th, the body of Galway's missing curate was accidentally discovered in a bog just off the Old Road to Galway above the village of Barna.

His remains were placed in a cart and taken to St. Joseph's Church in the city. It was at Mass the following morning that church officials told the public of Fr. Griffin's death. Galwegians grieved as details of the murdered priest's final hours were gradually discovered: he had died as a result of a gunshot wound to the head.

A funeral Mass was held on Tuesday, the 23rd, at St. Joseph's. Several thousand friends and community persons crowded into the church. The surrounding streets overflowed with mourners. Afterwards, his body was taken by motor car to Loughrea cathedral for burial. During the course of the journey, mourners lined the roads to the neighbouring town twenty-five miles away. The Irish people were saying their final farewells to a much-loved and highly respected priest.

A reconstruction of Father Griffin's final hours revealed that three men in civilian clothes had roused him from his bed. No doubt they were members of the British secret service. From his home, he was taken to Lenaboy Castle on Taylor's Hill, an Auxiliary Cadet headquarters. There he was tried, sentenced to death as a conspirator and shot in the back of the head. Later, his body was buried in a shallow, crudely dug bog grave.

Sure, on Friday, 14 November, pause as you pass along the road that bears his name or as you walk by the presbytery from which he was abducted. While doing so say a prayer for one of Ireland's and Galway's quiet but certainly not forgotten heroes. God bless you always, Father Griffin.

PEACE RISES FROM
IRISH ASHES...

PEACE RISES FROM
IRISH ASHES...

Maureen Dowd, syndicated columnist for the *New York Times*, penned a piece in late May, 1998 on Northern Ireland's April peace settlement and its overwhelming endorsement in May by Irish citizens, both north and south of the border. Entitled "Peace rises from Irish ashes," she praised the tireless efforts of President Bill Clinton and Prime Minister Tony Blair for their determination to break the Irish political logjam over peace in the Six Counties. Dowd stated, "With their youth and middle-class backgrounds, Mr. Clinton and Mr. Blair were not bound, as many American and British leaders before them, by World War II experiences or romantic notions of Empire and Pimm's Cup."

The Good Friday Peace Accord, finalised on Good Friday morning, 10 April 1998, had the real potential of bringing a lasting peace to the island of Ireland. Taken in its totality, the document, agreed to by all the major political parties in Northern Ireland as well as the British and Irish governments, represented the dawning of a new day in this war-torn part of Ireland and Great Britain.

On an optimistic note, Ms. Dowd observed, taking a cue from poet W. B. Yeats, "It appears that Northern Ireland's stony heart has begun to melt, that the people here have finally broken their cycle of fatalism, trading darkness for light, past for future."

On 22 May, a little over one month after the agreement was reached, Ireland went to the polls. It overwhelmingly supported the Good Friday 'Belfast Agreement.' Ninety-four percent of the voters in the Republic and seventy-one percent of the electorate of Northern Ireland endorsed it. A new chapter in Irish history had begun.

My response to this new Irish beginning and to Ms. Dowd's column appeared on the editorial opinion page of *The Cincinnati Enquirer* (Cincinnati, Ohio) in its 12 June 1998 issue, entitled "Ordinary people vote for peace in Ireland."

PEACE RISES FROM IRISH ASHES... *New York Times* columnist Maureen Dowd (27 May 1998) is certainly correct...British Prime Minister Tony Blair, American President Bill Clinton and Irish Prime Minister Bertie Ahern (not mentioned) deserve our gratitude and appreciation for a job well done. A task long overdue, no thanks to former British Prime Ministers Margaret Thatcher and John Major as well as former American Presidents Ronald Reagan and George Bush, Sr. If only those four past politicos had had the determination and will to foster peace in Northern Ireland (NI) as their successors have, thousands of lives and millions of pounds of property might have been spared.

But contrary to Ms. Dowd's view, the real catalyst in this matter was the Irish people themselves. It was the farmer, the shopkeeper, the housewife, the ordinary person in the streets of Northern Ireland who had had enough. The cry of peace was theirs. They were the ones who had elected nationalist John Hume, republican Gerry Adams, and unionist David Trimble. They were the ones who had wanted a life free of terror and violence. They were the underlying and driving force behind the political decisions of Good Friday. It is to them that we owe a great vote of thanks.

Through all the glad-handing and hope, however, there is much to do. One of the first steps must be David Trimble's.

After all those months of talk and negotiations, he must find the courage within himself to look Gerry Adams in the eye, to shake his hand and to work with him as an equal. For isn't that what the people wanted…a peaceful land where Northern Ireland's two traditions are embraced and celebrated in the true spirit of the Good Friday agreement?

BOG DAYS REMEMBERED...

BOG DAYS REMEMBERED...

This remembrance was first composed in 1996 and has been revised several times. It was inspired by a visit with Eileen and Tom Wright to a part of the great Bog of Allen in Ireland's midland near the village of Ferbane, Co. Offaly. For their kindness and friendship, I am eternally grateful.

The story first appeared in black and white in the *Offaly Independent* (Tullamore, Ireland) in 1997. A somewhat altered account was later printed in the May 2001 issue of the *Irish Midwest News* (Columbus, Ohio).

Bogs in Ireland are a post-glacial phenomenon (c. 8,000 B.C.), and once covered about one-seventh of Ireland's approximately 20,000,000-acre landmass. Classified as either blanket or raised bogs, they limited the development of Irish terra firma in early times. With the advent of more modern drainage schemes, however, peat bogs have become a source of arable land and fuel. Blanket bogs are found in more hilly or mountainous regions while raised bogs dominate in low-lying areas, especially in Ireland's Midland.

The Bog of Allen was formed as glaciated lakes slowly filled with soil runoff and new vegetation growth. Gradually, fens and marshes emerged, populated by acidic plant-life such as sphagnum moss. As this swampy land began drying out, hillocks emerged, attracting the growth of heathers. Between these bits of raised ground, pools of water remained, acting as a magnet for the further growth of more mosses. This repeated process of underwater decay and plant propagation eventually resulted in the formation of raised bogs, whose health and future growth, of course, depend on continual rainfall and repeated plant decay.

For hundreds of years the Irish have relied on the harvesting of bogs for a valuable commodity: peat or, as the Irish call it, turf.

Turbary rights, the right to dig turf on your own parcel of ground for domestic fuel use, was an important part of the old landlord-tenant relationship. These rights of turbary survive to this day, along with the more recent utilisation of peat for horticultural and industrial fuel usage.

The state-owned production of peat as a commercial fuel and generator of hydroelectric power began in 1946 with the formation of Bord na Mona. They sell much of their harvest to the Electricity Supply Board for the powering of energy-producing turbines. Also, bales of their processed turf briquettes can be purchased inexpensively at local shops. Thus, city dwellers, who have little access to a bog, may enjoy burning a bit of turf in their home fireplaces.

BOG DAYS REMEMBERED... With the coming of spring, the Clonmacnoise & West Offaly Railroad, near the village of Shannonbridge, Co. Offaly, will re-emerge from its winter hibernation for yet another year. From April through October, this unique train, operated by Bord na Mona as a tourist and educational attraction, travels over a small section of Ireland's huge Midland Bog of Allen that today is lined with over one hundred miles of narrow gauge railroad track. In addition to its sightseeing appeal, these rails provide a vital link between the mechanised monsters that harvest Ireland's carbon-rich soil (peat/turf) and its neighbouring Shannon River power plant. It is the burning of this unique harvest that fuels the plant's furnaces which are used to generate electricity.

Last autumn, as I sat back in the bog train's little tourist carriage, enjoying a warm afternoon, I was reminded of my youth and of some wonderful days spent in the bog near our home in the west of Ireland. Fifty years ago when jobs were scarce and money even more so, a few precious summer days were carved out of father's work-a-day life for the annual family 'saving of the turf.'

Around Dublin and down the southeast, coal and wood served as the primary domestic fuel. But for most of the people living along Ireland's Atlantic coast, it was turf that was used to cook our food and heat our homes. Yes, the acidic aroma of burning coal is distinctive, but the sweet smell of a turf fire is forever unforgettable. Its lingering scent is still as lovely as any Paris perfume or Sunday roast. For down through the years, it is a turf fire that is associated with home, hearth and happiness for countless thousands of Irish families.

As I reflected on those days gone by, I recalled that as June neared, my father eagerly listened to weather reports on the family's wireless in our sitting room. At last, when the forecast was favourable, we made plans for heading out to our generations-old family plot in the nearby bog. It was time to cut the turf again.

On the appointed day, we were all up early. My mother and sister organised a big breakfast fry and made plans for the day's other repasts. After our grand meal was finished, my father, two brothers and I headed off for a day of hard but much anticipated work.

First, the heather, grass and flower-bedecked top layer of soil was carefully removed. It was saved to recover the newly exposed earth after our annual digging was completed. With their angled slanes, Pa and my eldest brother began cutting the spongy, wet turf a board (row) at a time. By the end of the third day, only their heads would be visible as the eighty-foot-long and ever-widening excavation sank deeper and deeper into the bowels of the bog.

From the blades of their spade-like tools, they would throw huge, wet sods of quivering turf over to us. My younger brother and I would catch and stack the slippery masses onto our sideless, wooden barrow. After the load was carefully arranged, I would wheel it back toward the laneway, dumping its precious cargo onto the bog's flat, grassy surface. We then carefully arranged the soggy rectangles to form a single layer of sod blocks, each exposed to the drying forces of summer's sun and its warm breezes.

This demanding but fondly remembered toil filled the next several days from morning 'til late evening. Though the work was back-breaking, it was shortened by many wonderful songs and countless old stories, fondly told and retold.

In addition to these simple pleasures, my mother and sister would arrive about ten o'clock in the morning to make 'bog tea' for us. An old heavily-blackened kettle, filled with fresh spring water, was put to boil on a fire made from the scattered remains of last year's dried bits of turf. The smoke from these sods gave the tea a unique and unforgettable flavour. Accompanying the tea were thick cuts of homemade brown bread smeared with lashings of fresh butter and blackcurrant jam. This short pause in our labours was filled with more songs and some of father's oft repeated poetry. Then, just as the warmth and goodness of the refreshment was beginning to ease our aching muscles, Pa would announce it was time to 'get on with it.'

At half one, more bread and tea arrived into the bog. This time, however, it was accompanied by eggs boiled in an old bean tin plus hot jacketed spuds topped off with lots of fresh sweet butter. Finally, toward evening, my sister brought us one last round of nourishment. Our seven o'clock tea, biscuits and, if we were lucky, a custard-like pudding signalled our day's toiling would be soon over.

After a winter's worth of fuel was cut and spread out over the top of the bog, we let the sods dry for several weeks. To hint that this vital process had begun, our earthen blocks would begin growing a thin crusty 'skin' on their upturned sides.

Over the next few weeks our family periodically returned to the bog to further facilitate this desiccating process. We would turn over the drying sods to expose yet another surface to the dehydrating warmth of the sun.

If the weather stayed fair, we would all be back five or six weeks later to undertake yet another step in this summer-long devotion to duty. Working in teams of two, the family stacked the hardening bricks into footings. These small hive-like structures consisted of eight carefully arranged sods that allowed for increased air circulation around the blocks, all helping to speed up the drying time.

Later on, toward the end of July, just before the autumn harvest began, the now hardened bricks of sod were loaded into a horse-drawn wagon and driven home. Next, our precious fuel was restacked, this time into a large reek. This trapezoidal mound would be six or eight feet wide at its base while the sloped sides would stand four or five feet in height. Depending on the success of our endeavours, the family's newly built turf reek stretched along the ground for what seemed to me to be a great distance. Finally, an old tarpaulin was spread over the reek and anchored down. It would keep all manners of weather from attacking the newly harvested sods.

Yes, it is with fond memories that I remember back to those days of hard work and to the summer's endless hours of turning, stacking and hauling. But our family labour of love did have a happy ending. As the cold winds of winter lashed against the house, our home was kept delightfully warm and pleasantly filled with the sweet aroma of mother's home cooking and the burning turf...all thanks to the great bog and its centuries-old gift of cherished fuel.

ALONG FREEDOM'S ROAD...

ALONG FREEDOM'S ROAD...

I wrote this story in response to a visit to Ireland during the summer of 2001. It appeared in its entirety in the August, 2001 issue of the *Midwest Irish News* (Columbus, Ohio). A portion of it was also published in the *Irish Echo* (New York City) at the end of January, 2002.

In the short time I had been away, the changes in Ireland seemed so dramatic to me. Sure since the early 1990s, the influences of European Union money, increased tourism, the coming of age of Ireland's economically roaring Celtic Tiger, inexpensive mobile telephones, the advent of the Internet plus the influx of satellite-directed television programmes have all had a major impact in accelerating the rate of change in Irish life.

Eamon de Valera must be turning over in his grave. Gone forever are the days of comely maidens dancing at the crossroads and Irish farm families living in simple, frugal comfort. That rural Ireland of Dev's yesterday is but a distant memory today.

The poem *GOING HOME* was written in the summer of 1994.

ALONG FREEDOM'S ROAD...Signs of Ireland's newfound prosperity abound. Evidence of a building boom is everywhere. Dublin streets, the ones not closed due to road works that is, are overflowing with people, cars, lorries and buses of all sorts. There are fewer bicycles and more Mercedes and BMWs. Down the country the roads seem better but the traffic volume is up. There are more 'blow-ins' than ever before. I have never seen more fifty-punt banknotes being passed in shops and credit cards being used for even the smallest of purchases. Mobile telephones abound. That small crowd in front of the pub is not waiting to gain entrance. They have left their pints on the table inside for better telephonic reception outside. The national question is not what happened in the Six Counties today, but rather how do we get our 'mattress money' in circulation without the tax man finding out about it. (Ireland is joining the European Union Monetary System on 1 January 2002. All Irish punts must be converted to Euros by the end of February.) Ireland is changing, changing fast, and I am not one who welcomes it with open arms.

All that aside, history is still alive and well in Ireland. Yesterday was just moments ago and the past is within memory's reach, if you choose to think about it. So recently, on a fine summer's day, I headed my rented blue Fiat northeast out of Clonmel (Co. Tipperary) onto the Kilkenny Road (N76). Skirting Slievenamon, I took a brief detour up a narrow side road to have a closer look at Kilcash Castle. Being of no great national interest, this massive decaying tower house and simple nearby church are not mentioned in any of the popular tour literature. Today, however, they are a majestic reminder of an Ireland five hundred years ago. Their silent crumbling stones still keep watch over the grassy fields running up to the Comeragh Mountains and Booley Hills beyond.

Further along at the Ballymack crossroads is a signpost for The Warhouse and The Commons. If you are a history buff or a nationalist at heart take the diversion. (This narrow road will test your left-hand driving skills to be sure, but just slow down and not to worry, the drive is one you will survive.)

One-and-a-half miles beyond the village of Ballingarry, up a narrow boreen, are the Widow McCormack's cottage and cabbage patch...the scene of the Rebellion of 1848. The are no cabbages to be found today, but the thatched cottage has been newly restored in striking detail. It is well worth a visit.

It was here on 29 July 1848 that the Young Islanders engaged the forces of the Crown. It was the only battle of that famine-ravaged uprising. As the story goes, the Young Islanders rendezvoused on the 28th at The Commons, a crossroads one-mile from the fateful house. It was at this crossing, as history records, Thomas Francis Meagher (pronounced Maher) presented the tricolour to the Irish people. His words are there for all to read in that wee hamlet. "The white in the centre signifies a lasting truce between the Orange and the Green, and I trust that beneath its folds the hand of the Irish Protestant and the Irish Catholic may be clasped in generous and heroic brotherhood." Atop the modest monument at The Commons, the Irish flag has flown ever since.

After the fatal cottage standoff on the 29th, the Young Islanders were forced to flee, exiled to the ends of the earth. But it was there on that hollowed ground that the likes of William Smith O'Brien, John Blake Dillon, Terence Bellew MacManus, James Stephens, John O'Mahony, Michael Doheny, Maurice Richard Leyne, James Cantwell, Patrick O'Donohue, Thomas Devin Reilly, Meagher and others fought together for Ireland's freedom.

Farther on out of Kilkenny Town take the Carlow road (N9). From there head east to Tullow (R725). Visit the monument to 1798 heroes Father John Murphy, priest and patriot, and his faithful follower, John Gallagher. For it was there on a hot July day in 'The Year of Liberty' that these two men were half-hanged and then burned to death in tar barrels. Their stone inscription states that the two "...were most cruelly and barbarously put to death by English soldiers on the square of Tullow in 1798. God Save Ireland."

Back behind the wheel, follow the main road (N81) to Baltinglass. Stop for a bite to eat at one of two nice hotels facing the town square. Both serve a lovely carvery lunch with several choices of hand-carved meat, spuds, veg and a sweet treat to top off your dining pleasure.

On the square again, take a moment to remember the stories of the legendary Michael Dwyer and his loyal comrade, Sam MacAllister, who gave his life so his friend might live. The monument in the town centre is dedicated to these 1798 heroes. It depicts Dwyer holding his famous blunderbuss by his side. In addition, the statue honours seven of Dwyer's men who were arrested and executed by the Stranger in 1799 on the very spot just before you.

Two final side trips, both well worth a visit, but not found in the guidebooks, are the Dwyer cottage where he and his followers had it out with the English on 15 February 1799 and Dunlavin Green.

The Dwyer-English engagement is known by the locals as the Battle of Doire-na-Muc. The cottage is in the beautiful Glen of Imaal about two miles from the tiny village of Knockanarrigan. The roads leading up into the hills are narrow, but the view of the Wicklow Mountains is like none you have ever seen...breathtaking indeed. It was in the cottage that the wounded MacAllister drew the enemy's fire to himself so that Dwyer could slip out the door and escape. The Irishman gave his life so his friend might live and fight another day.

The second spot is the village green in Dunlavin, a lovely village about six miles northwest off the main road to Hollywood. Besides some unusual architecture, this is the infamous spot where on 24 May 1798 thirty-six United Irishmen were massacred...shot to death as they knelt before His Majesty's forces. As the song *Dunlavin Green* reminds us, "...when the blood ran in streams down the dykes of Dunlavin Green."

Yes, the past is alive and well in old Ireland, despite all of 'Progress's' changing ways.

GOING HOME

Long years he had waited to cross that wide sea,
He'd dreamt of his homeland, not else could there be;
Each night after work as he turned out the light,
He remembered the sun on the sea shining bright.
Oh hills of green grass, golden heather in bloom,
And the granite grey walls of his ancient Macroom;
That town of his youth he had known long ago,
Now soon he'd be home, not much time left to go.

The sweet Shannon air was washed clean by the wind,
He was back in dear Ireland, so long it had been,
That his eyes overflowed with memory-filled tears;
Would his old friends remember after all of those years?
He had written, sent pictures, even rung on the phone,
But now 'twas all different as he drove the road home;
The sadness he knew when he felt his heart race,
There wasn't much time and so much to retrace.

He drove to the pub...all his friends would be there,
Their music and laughter and smoke filled the air;
As their hands reached out and old mates he embraced,
All the years in between seemed to melt with such haste,
It was as if he'd stayed home and had never been gone.
Had time stood still? Was it a dream all along?
Then the pain is his chest reminded him that,
He hadn't much longer to linger and chat.

Donning his cap and finishing his beer,
He said his good-byes in a voiced masked with cheer;
Promising to return, he walked to the door,
But his time it had come, he'd not have any more...
His friends found him next morning as they walked up
   to Mass,
The note that he clutched in his hand was his last;
'Won't ye bury me up on the hill by me home,
For I love this dear land and no more will I roam.'

SLAINTE!...

SLAINTE!...

The following was written in 1998, in response to what seemed like hundreds of requests by tourists I met, while leading city tours around Galway, and by acquaintances in the States who wanted suggestions for pubs to visit while on holiday in Ireland.

Under no circumstances was it ever intended to be a comprehensive guidebook on 'the pubs of Ireland.' Rather it was based on one person's experiences, mine, vis-à-vis some interesting and pleasurable places to enjoy 'the odd pint.'

If you were interested in something more expansive, I would suggest looking in the back of some internationally known tour guides or browsing through a bookshop, preferably in Ireland, for paperbacks on Irish pubs. There are several to choose from that should satisfy most needs. Then of course, there is always the Internet for those of you who have joined 'the computer age.'

Unfortunately, Ireland, to my knowledge, has no equivalent to Britain's outstanding pub guide entitled *The Good Pub Guide, 2003*. It contains a wealth of information in its over 1,000 pages and is still edited by its originator, Alisdair Aird. Besides its detailed ratings, beer descriptions, historical vignettes and charming details, this astonishing tome, annually updated since 1983, has many excellent maps, making the most out-of-the-way rural pub easier to find. Its mind-boggling list of over 1,300 public houses in England, Scotland, Wales and the Channel Islands is a great read and a brilliant travelling companion. I have known people who kept a copy in their automobile's glove box, ticking off the places they have visited while comparing notes with Alisdair. It is so comprehensive you could use it as your sole guide for motoring around Britain, that is if you like beer, skittles and pub food.

"Slainte!" is the Irish word for health. Pronounced SH-LAwn-ta, its pub translation would be "to your health!" or "Good health!" or, if you are English or from Boston, "Cheers!" An Irish reply to 'slainte' might be 'slainte mhaith' (SH-LAwn-ta wa) meaning "Good health to you!"

SLAINTE!...James Joyce's wonderful Ulysses character, Leopold Bloom mused, "A good puzzle would be to cross Dublin without passing a pub." The answer to Bloom's conundrum is, of course, why pass a pub. Just go inside each one you encounter and enjoy yourself. Then leave by the rear door. That way you never actually passed the pub by.

Pubs or public houses in Ireland are a way of life. They are as old and as timeless as the Irish themselves. There are thousands of them. Some wee ones are tucked away in the nooks and crannies of rural Ireland. In the major towns, some are big, bold and brassy. Most fall somewhere in between the two extremes. The last number I heard was in excess of eleven thousand pubs in Ireland. That is a good few for a country the size of West Virginia or Oregon.

Pubs are an extension of your own sitting room. A communal neighbourhood gathering place for the entire family: your own social club just down the way. A place to meet the 'locals.' Great spots for 'people watching.' Their often quaint interiors offer the visitor inexpensive food and drink, a dry spot out of the damp and, if you are lucky, a warm fire to cosy up to as you enjoy some Irish music or a song. Pubs are the dens of the storyteller and backdrops for shared friendships or budding romances. They are homes away from home. Public houses in Ireland are keepers of the Irish spirit. They are places to revere, to appreciate and, most of all, to enjoy. Customarily, publicans are one of the most respected and honoured members of the local community. Their word carries extra weight and their advice is often sought in resolving matters. Especially in rural Ireland, the stature of a publican in traditional Irish society is not far below that of the parish priest.

If you enjoy a bit of craic (an Irish good time) and the occasional 'wee drop' or are a confirmed teetotaller, these hostelries of homeyness are not to be missed. Sure they must be so, or why are they being reinvented in countries all around the world today?

Some of the best stories I know were bar banter overheard in pubs. Besides comfort and refreshment, pubs are great places to inquire about where to go and what to do next. Just ask the publican, barman or the person sitting next to you for a suggestion. Fifteen minutes later you will have a list of half-a-dozen destinations that are not found in any tour book. Indeed, from the simplest, most remote shebeen in Connemara to the finest, most elegant bar in the best Dublin hotel, pubs are part and parcel of Irish culture, its people and history.

Unfortunately, there is a downside to all this great ambiance. Pubs are usually smoky; sometimes crowded, especially the good ones after half ten at night when it is difficult to squeeze up to the bar for a refill; and the busy ones can be noisy. When this happens, you might hear the person next to you complain, "I'll be after leaving you in the grace of God for there's no comfort to be had in here so!" Other than that, what is there to grumble about?

I offer a few odd bits and pieces of information that may come in handy for the uninitiated traveller. These are generalisations that might vary from time to time and place to place, so good luck. Irish pubs do not run tabs. You pay when each order is served. Tipping is not expected, but as you leave, especially if some special service has been provided, a coin or two left on the bar or table is always appreciated. If the place is crowded, expect to be asked by strangers to share a table. Do not be afraid to strike up a conversation with the person next to you. Most Irish do have the gift of gab and a 'foreigner' in their midst stirs the curiosity. The Irish serve what Americans call 'mixed drinks' with little ice, but feel free to ask for another cube or two. Gin and tonics come with a lemon slice, not lime. All pubs offer a range of inexpensive bottled waters, still or sparkling. You are not thought to be someone out of the ordinary if you order one. The Irish drink their beverages out of glasses, not bottles. In my biased opinion, this age-old custom is changing among the younger generation...thanks to the influence of satellite telly programmes and Ireland's growing Americanisation.

Here are a couple of Irish drinking customs you should be aware of that might keep you from being caught off guard or trapped. Often a person enters a pub looking to have one drink. Being a friendly sort, he joins a group of three or four acquaintances. Someone in the quartet buys a round. Now, instead of paying for and having just one drink, your man is socially obligated to pay for and have three or four drinks. It is called being 'in a round.' So, if you find yourself in a group, be clear about your wishes, or you may be overtaxing your limits and your pocketbook. Finally, if someone buys you a drink in Ireland, it is customary to return the favour. It is a courtesy, however, and not a requirement.

As you might have guessed, the Irish take their 'pints' seriously. Guinness, a dark, rich-tasting stout (an ale versus a lager), is the national drink. Some consume it by the pint while others order it by the glass (a half-pint). A good pint takes two, three maybe even four minutes to pour from the tap. (It only seems longer if you are thirsty.) Served at about fifty degrees Fahrenheit (about ten degrees Celsius), the pint glass is first filled three-quarters full, then allowed to settle. After a minute or two, more is added and again allowed to stand. Finally, it is topped off and served with a head about half-an-inch or so high that slightly exceeds the rim of the glass: proud of rim. After it is placed before you, it is customary to wait a few moments before drinking. Its black goodness should be completely free of any bubbles with its creamy head still perfectly formed. As the liquid is consumed, a 'good pint' will leave a velvety residue clinging to the inside of the glass. This remainder is called 'a ring.' A typical Irish Guinness drinker will leave five or six rings in an empty glass. This indicates the beverage was consumed in five or six good 'pulls' on the pint. Normally, a pint is savoured slowly...what is the rush? Guinness is not Ireland's only stout and its several breweries around the country produce a range of lagers as well. Foreign beers are available too. Heineken and Budweiser are two of the most popular alternatives. On a fine summer's day, an Irish shandy (part lager, part Irish lemonade) can hit the spot.

Two final thoughts on beer in Ireland. Contrary to the popular misconception, Irish tap beer is chilled, not served at room temperature. It is the small bottles of Guinness Extra Stout that are generally served warm. This is still a popular drink among 'gentlemen' of the 'older' generation, but its consumption is on the wane. Finally, there is much debate about which pub serves the best pint. Rather than try to explain what makes a 'good' pint good, I will leave it up to your own taste buds, but if you want to strike up a conversation with an Irishman and do not know where to start, just ask him, "What makes a good pint?" But only ask if you have half an hour or so to spare. Expect to pay about 3.70 euros per pint.

Now, I realise I am sticking me neck out and laying my reputation on the line by recommending pubs for others to

visit. Things are always shifting. Pubs come and go. Ownership changes. Staff moves on. Clientele fluctuates. So what is
true today may not be so tomorrow. One good thing about
Ireland, however, it that things change a bit more slowly,
except maybe in Dublin, than in the rest of the world. So
hopefully, there may still be some validity in these recom-
mendations.

DUBLIN TOWN:

> So many pubs to chose from, it is mind-boggling. A
> few of my very favourites, in no particular order, in-
> clude: **Doheny & Nesbitt**, 5 Lower Baggot Street, is a
> mid-nineteenth century pub and very popular; **The
> Palace Bar**, 21 Fleet Street, is an unblemished pub
> catering to the literary and newspaper crowd. The back
> room is lovely with its diffused light from the overhead
> milky skylight; a wonderful Victorian pub **The Stag's
> Head**, 1 Dame Court is hard to find but worth the
> effort. On Dame Street, take the cobble-stoned laneway
> through the arch opposite Crow Street to Dame Court.
> Ask for Francie, the barman; another Victorian gem
> full of history is **Toner's**, 139 Lower Baggot Street; the
> tiny **Foggy Dew**, 1 Fownes Street Upper; the elegant
> **Horseshoe Bar in the Shelbourne Hotel**, Stephen's
> Green; behind the back gate of Glasnevin Cemetery,
> **Kavanagh's**, 1 Prospect Square; and if you like the
> tourist crowd, the oldest pub in Dublin, 1688, is **The
> Brazen Head**, 20 Lower Bridge Street. Two others of
> special note: the once wonderful **The Bailey**, 2-3 Duke
> Street has been chopped up into wee bits and sold to
> Mark's & Spencer's (a British store!). What is left of the
> old place is still worth a look in. Close your eyes and
> imagine hearing the voices of Brendan Behan, Oliver
> St. John Gogarty, Paddy Kavanagh, Michael Collins or

the English voices of some Black & Tans (to mention only a few) holding forth. Lastly, on Friday nights a little after nine, head for the **Trinity Inn** on Pearse Street...Patrick and William Pearse of 1916 fame lived just down the street. Walk up the outside stairs, pay your punt/euro at the door, come in and take a seat. Be prepared for an extraordinary evening of traditional Irish entertainment and sharing, as the assembled group of eighty or so Dubliners entertain each other with songs, poetry and stories. This is the Ireland of a hundred years ago.

DOWN THE COUNTRY:

ADARE, Co. Limerick: Anglo-Irish sumptuousness **The Tack Room Bar in Adare Manor**, at the top of the town...

ANASCAUL, Co. Kerry: One of the most photographed pubs in Ireland is **Dan Foley's**. It sadly misses its gracious host and namesake...

ATHLONE, Co. Roscommon: A real work of art. Check out the ceiling above the bar. Nice outdoor beer garden for summer evenings. Next to the River Shannon in the old town just below the castle is **Sean's Bar**...

ATHY, Co. Kildare: A small country pub is **Des Noonan's** on the main street...

BALLYNAHINCH MANOR HOUSE, Co. Galway: Famous residence of Dick 'Trigger' Martin, MP; the lower level pub is something right out of the eighteenth century with a lovely restaurant upstairs. It is just off the road between Clifton & Recess...you may have to ask directions, but it is worth it...

BELFAST, Co. Antrim: The epitome of Victorian grandeur **The Crown Liquor Saloon** on Great Victoria Street is in the heart of the city...

CASTLETOWNBERE, Co. Cork: A wonderful country pub is **MacCarthy's**...

CLARINBRIDGE, Co. Galway: The oyster capital of Ireland is **Paddy Burke's** thatched pub on the main road to Galway...

DINGLE TOWN, Co. Kerry: Classic pubs not to be missed are **Dick Mack's** & **O'Flaherty's** in this charming wee town...

ENNIS TOWN, Co. Clare: At opposite ends of the town Daniel O'Connell made famous are **The Old Ground Hotel Bar**, next to the church at the top of the town & **The Cloister** on Abbey Street, next to the ruins at the bottom of the town...

FETHARD, Co. Tipperary: Old post office & grocery store cum pub is **McCarthy's**, Just on the main road through town and is Ireland a century ago...

GALWAY TOWN: Old-time pubs include **O'Connell's**, **Fibber McGee's** & **Garvey's** all facing Eyre Square and Kennedy Park; **Richardson's**, a traditional pub steeped in history with fine Irish sing-a-longs sung by the great Gabo Cooley, is hosted by the lovely Richardson family from Co. Tipperary. Tom Richardson is a fine historian with a no-nonsense approach to it; **The Snug/Garvan's** in Shop Street is another truly old pub patronised by 'interesting' people; another traditional classic pub is **Murphy's** in the High Street; a couple of doors down the way is **The Bunch of Grapes**, owned and operated by golfers Tom and Mary Corcoran &

family. It is a fine pub with a genteel air and is directly across the street from Kennys great bookshop. At 'The Bunch,' Mary's and Caroline's ham salad sandwiches are not to be missed; **The Quays**, on Quay Street is one of Galway's several huge pubs cum drinking salon and music hall. Built on a nautical theme, it is well worth a good look around and a pint as well; **Tigh Neachtain's**, 17 Cross Street, is known for its snugs (private high-backed booths) and its traditional music sessions. Be sure to ask for Eddie, the barman. He is a fount of information about Galway and a wonderful conversationalist as well...

KILCOLGAN, Co. Galway: **Moran's on the Weir** is just off the main Galway-Gort Road. This cottage pub serves lovely seafood and specialises in fresh oysters caught just a few feet from its front door...

KILKENNY TOWN: the oft-time, award-winning **Langton's**, 69 John Street...

KILLARNEY, Co. Kerry: Just across from the gates of Muckross National Park, the thatched-roofed **Molly D'Arcy's** retraces Ireland's fight for freedom in pictures...

LIMERICK: Next to Bunratty Castle the touristy **Durty Nellie's**, near Shannon Airport, serves a nice pint and surprisingly good food...

LISTOWEL, Co. Kerry: Son Jimmy, who also writes, now runs the joint after the recent death (May, 2002) of his famous writer-father **John B. Keane**. The small, homey family pub is located in the heart of the town...

ROUNDWOOD, Co. Wicklow: Lovely food and a country pub, **The Roundwood Inn** is on the main road through town...

THURLES, Co. Tipperary: **The Hayes Hotel** is the site where the Gaelic Athletic Association was founded in 1884 by Michael Cusack. It is on the town's main street...

WESTPORT, Co. Mayo: Home and musical pub of Matt Molloy of The Chieftains fame is aptly named **Matt Molloy's**. Needless to say, it is a great place to enjoy some fine Irish music...

...and this humble listing does not even scratch the surface. I simply urge the curious traveller to be adventurous, strike out on your own and sample the pubs that look inviting to you...they probably will be. Jot down the names of the places you enjoy and make a few notes to yourself. That way you can tell your friends all about the pubs of Ireland...the ones you found interesting that is...just as I have done. Slainte!

THE SPIRIT OF
GOOD FRIDAY...

THE SPIRIT OF
GOOD FRIDAY...

Los Angeles Times writer, Marjorie Miller, commented on the political evolution taking place in Northern Ireland (NI) in her June, 1998 story entitled, "Trimble ready to carry burden of Assembly." New York City's *Irish Echo* also carried several narratives on the same subject.

For a change, these news stories emanating from Northern Ireland were positive ones. They described and analysed the most recent steps taken by Belfast's emerging government born of the April, 1998 Good Friday Agreement.

On 25 June 1998, hundreds of thousands of Northern Irish voters took to the polls, electing a new Assembly for the Six Counties. This was the third step in an ongoing process outlined in the recent Belfast Accord, signed on Good Friday, 1998. First, the leaders of all major Northern Irish political parties reached concurrence on the document in April. This was followed by an island-wide referendum in May, endorsing the terms of the eleven-section agreement. Now in June, it was time to elect representatives to the newly created 108-member NI Assembly.

The results of the election were predictable with only a few surprises to raise the pundits' eyebrows. Though seventy-one percent of the total Northern Irish population, voting in the May referendum, supported the Agreement, only fifty-five percent of the unionist community favoured the document. Approximately ninety-five percent of the North's nationalists gave the thumbs-up sign to the deal. Thus, a big question arose: would the narrow margin of unionist voters continue to support the new Assembly, or would political infighting, so common in NI, erode the spirit and effectiveness of the new body? Early indications from the June election indicated that the latter would probably be the case.

Catholic and cross-border nationalists were in favour of the agreement, electing fifty representatives to the Assembly. John Hume, the moderate nationalist leader of the Social Democratic and Labour Party, and Gerry Adams, president of republican Sinn Fein, were the heads of their contingents at that time. Hume has since retired and was recently replaced by Mark Durkin.

The Ulster Unionist Party, headed by David Trimble, garnered the most seats of any party, twenty-eight, and was joined on the pro-agreement side of the table by the Progressive Unionist Party. Together they formed a bloc of thirty. The surprise was that Trimble's UUP received the lowest vote in the party's history while Sinn Fein and the Democratic Unionist Party (DUP) showed strong growth. It is not hard to imagine a future marked by Adams and Ian Paisley going head to head over the key issues.

Co-1998 Nobel peace prize winner David Trimble (shared with fellow Ulsterman John Hume) was selected First Minister, owing to his party's having garnered the greatest number of all seats.

Opposition came in the form of twenty-eight seats won by the anti-agreement parties. Headed by Reverend Paisley's DUP (20 seats), the United Kingdom Unionist Party (5 seats) and independents (3 seats), this coalition of assembly members possessed a major threat to the success and effectiveness of the new Assembly.

In her piece, *L.A. Times* writer Marjorie Miller prophetically noted back in 1998, "But it is not clear whether the advocates of change will be strong enough to guarantee the success of the 108-member Assembly and the survival of the bullets-to-ballots peace process."

Unfortunately, her pessimism has proven true over the past four and a half years. The Northern Irish Assembly has been racked with discord and dissension.

In a letter-to-the-editor of the *Irish Echo*, dated 8 July 1998, I shared Ms. Miller's concern. The headline over my comment was, "An Orange threat to peace remains."

THE SPIRIT OF GOOD FRIDAY...The hopeful spirit of the Good Friday peace agreement moved one step closer to reality this past weekend. The accord, signed April last by negotiators on behalf of the Irish people, both north and south plus their respective London and Dublin governments, continues limping down the peace path.

In May, Ireland's citizens overwhelmingly voted to support the terms of the Anglo-Irish treaty. Then, last Friday, the people of Northern Ireland (NI) chose their representatives to fill Stormont's seats, empty since the spring of 1972 when Westminster prorogued its Belfast government. But now, a new vocal minority is revolting, vowing to do all it can to disrupt the burgeoning democracy, as life in NI comes full circle.

For the past three hundred and eighty years, it was largely a powerless Catholic underclass that cried out. The target of economic and political unionist persecution, they were forcibly evicted from their land, burned out of their homes, denied fair employment or adequate housing, gerrymandered at the ballot box, subjected to unlawful arrest and denied due process by the judicial system. Yes, the Catholic and nationalist community endured much. Today, however, a stalwartly sonorous element, this time mostly Protestant and unionist, is crying foul.

The extremists, led by the Reverend Ian Paisley and others, seemingly fearful of losing their often illegally gained advantage, doggedly remain tied to the past while denying the yoke of honest self-government. As peace and justice finally seep through the cracks in the floorboards of Northern

Ireland, this group apparently fears the hand of righteous retribution. All this while NI prepares to stand up and be democratically counted for the first time in history.

Sadly, the bloodshed in Ireland is not over with yet as another 'marching season' approaches. The Orange Order, with its two centuries of militant, sectarian determination, continues to defy sanity. But it is the hope of all peace-loving people, nationalists and unionists alike, that Ireland can withstand this summer's bitter blast, emerging stronger and more united than ever before.

'TIS THE MARCHING SEASON IN IRELAND...

'TIS THE MARCHING
SEASON IN IRELAND...

The lead editorial in *The Cincinnati Enquirer* of 9 July 1998 stated boldly, "Obstinate refusal to confer keeps compromise at bay."

The column noted that the new Northern Irish Assembly "...took sensible action with the summer parade season heating up: It recessed till mid-September."

Wishing not to become embroiled in the annual heated controversy over whether Protestant Orange Order parades should be allowed to march through Catholic nationalist neighbourhoods, the month-old governing body wisely decided this was not the time to test its fledgling powers.

Even with the support of 30,000 British troops to augment the work of Northern Ireland's police force, local agencies have a difficult time preventing sectarian clashes over the right of the Orange Order to march where and when they wish. The celebration of the 1690 victory of Protestant King William III over Catholic King James II at the Battle of the Boyne on July 12th (N.S.) is the highlight of the Protestant calendar in the North.

Needless to day, Catholics continually demand that their communities not be subjected to the rampant triumphant provocations that resonate from these yearly street celebrations. Too often homes or shops are destroyed and individuals are injured or killed, as loyalist celebrants parade through nationalist areas of Northern Ireland. In support of this claim, the newspaper editorial mentioned that the outlawed pro-British Loyalist Volunteer Force had recently burned ten Catholic churches in the Six Counties.

Thankfully, these flash points are few in number, but tend to be concentrated during the months of July and August each year.

Annually, there are more than 2,000 Orange Order parades with only ten percent of them contentious and newsworthy. The Garvaghy Road in Portadown, Co. Armagh, the Apprentice Boys Parade in Derry City and the Ormeau Road parade in Belfast are the major offenders.

Loyalist harassment of Catholics, however, is not restricted to the marching season. Prime examples of radical sectarianism that recently made the newspaper headlines include the tormenting of churchgoers at a local Catholic church in Ballymena, Co. Antrim, and the ongoing harassment of students and their parents at the girls' Holy Cross Primary School in North Belfast. It is hard to fathom what satisfaction is gained from these bigoted outbursts.

Finally, the editorial pointed out that "...the days of unionist domination in the North are waning." It cited the example that a Catholic is mayor of Belfast. (Today, Alex Maskey, a member of Sinn Fein, is Belfast's mayor.) *The Enquirer* went on to mention that David Trimble was preaching calm back in the summer of 1998, but was labelled a 'traitor' by hard-line unionists. Ian Paisley had vowed to wreck the Assembly that autumn, but denounced the ten Catholic church burnings.

And so it goes. Change is deliberate in Northern Ireland. Hatred and political favour are slow to die. Hopefully, the Good Friday Peace Accord will finally open the door to a new tomorrow in the North.

The following, written on the eve of the July 12th celebrations in 1998, was in response to the *Enquirer* editorial.

'TIS THE MARCHING SEASON IN IRELAND...Life in Ireland has never been easily understood by outsiders. On the Emerald Isle today the past is ever alive. Yesterday's historical figures still 'live' next door. The contrasts between Ireland's two traditions—Catholic & Protestant, nationalist & unionist, republican & loyalist—again fly at us through the media. Life in Ireland evolves ever so slowly.

At the moment, it is the unionist community's turn in Northern Ireland to don the label 'rebel,' as one element within their lot, the right-wing Orange Order, becomes the bullyboy, the cudgel carrier and the thug. Refusing to mediate with their Catholic neighbours, the Orange lodgers demand their hereditary right to march, using threats to lever their way through what have now become nationalist Catholic areas. Just this week in the rural village of Dunloy, Co. Antrim, Orangemen surrounded its Catholic community, terrorising and threatening to inflict their own brand of righteous justice upon its tiny populace.

All of this posturing and violence in the Six Counties is symptomatic of the division within unionist society today. The ratification of the Good Friday Peace Accord threatens their heritage and culture. They fear their often illegally gained freedoms are slowly eroding.

With the major paramilitary parties on both sides declaring cease-fires months ago, a limited peace has existed in the North. But, as there is no common understanding or agreement within those elements, radical splinter groups are always in danger of taking action into their own hands. Hints of meaningful change are in the air, but true reconciliation must include everyone if it is to have any real meaning.

Does this latest outburst over the marching season mark the beginning of the end of a two-centuries-old unionist stranglehold on Northern Ireland, or will it simply result in a new escalation of sectarian violence with unfathomable consequences for all?

OH, NO!
OMAGH!...

OH, NO! OMAGH!...

On Saturday afternoon, 15 August 1998, members of the Real IRA (Irish Republican Army) detonated a five-hundred-pound device on Market Street in Omagh, Co. Tyrone. The town's main shopping area was crowded with weekend shoppers. The results were catastrophic. Twenty-eight people, both Catholic and Protestant, were killed outright. One more died later in hospital. Of the dead, fourteen were women; seven were children. Three generations of one family were killed in the blast. It was the worst single act of violence in the 'Ulster War' that dates back to the late 1960s. Minutes before the explosion, the local newspaper received a telephone call. It warned that a car bomb had been planted close to the courthouse, near the town centre. In response, the authorities began herding people away from the building toward the market square.

Whether by error or on purpose, the warning of the bomb's location was wrong. It was not adjacent to the courthouse, but nearer to the main shopping district. People were actually crowding toward, not away from, the danger, making the destruction even more devastating.

The Real IRA was formed in late 1997-early 1998 when approximately thirty disaffected members of the Provisional IRA (PIRA) decided to go it alone. Politically aligned with the 32-County Sovereignty Committee, these men and women disagreed with the PIRA's willingness to go along with Sinn Fein's participation in the on-going peace talks and that political party's possible membership in the newly planned Northern Irish assembly. These breakaway republicans felt participation in the talks was a betrayal of past Irish republicans, who had died for the right of Irish independence and self-determination.

As a direct result of the Omagh tragedy, two republican splinter groups, the Irish National Liberation Army and the offending Real IRA, declared cease-fires, ending their active paramilitary manoeuvres. Additionally, several weeks later Gerry Adams, President of Sinn Fein, in an historic declaration stated that violence in the North must come to an end, that it was a thing of the past. Adams also added that it [violence] must be over and done with...now! The authorities in Northern Ireland are still investigating the Omagh bombing incident.

OH, NO! OMAGH!...Being Irish, it was not easy waking up this Sunday morning, considering what happened yesterday. The headlines and telly all scream the news...at least twenty-eight dead and more than two hundred injured. My country's men and women are killing each other again. I am shocked and ashamed of their murderous behaviour. The bombing in Omagh was an act of unconscionable cowardice and totally without merit.

I am assuming the news reports are correct when they state that a splinter republican paramilitary group is responsible. Opposed to the IRA's cease-fire and participation in the peace process, either the Irish National Liberation Army or the 32 County-Real IRA is most likely responsible for the attack. There is always, however, a shadow of doubt in my mind about who is really to blame for such things. I can remember numerous times when loyalist paramilitary or British undercover SAS (Special Air Service) units have staged attacks, hoping their republican counterparts would be tagged with the blame...but I somehow doubt it this time.

In Ireland the past dies hard. There have been too many terribly tragic and unforgettable episodes. For over eight hundred years Ireland has been overrun, violated and occupied by 'the Stranger' from England. Now, however, with hope on the horizon, things may change. Peace, self-government and maybe even Irish unity are in sight. Unfortunately, though, small elements within Northern Ireland (NI) refuse to accept peace through negotiation. They maintain their rigid adherence to violence in order to bring about their desired objectives: driving the 'Brits' out and uniting Ireland, or maintaining unionist status quo.

Today, all splinter groups are under tremendous pressure from the Royal Ulster Constabulary. This NI police force, aided by London's MI5, the British Army and key Dublin governmental units, are breathing down their necks. Recently, the INLA was unable to pull off a limited bombing campaign in Britain, aimed at crippling its economy. Today, 'republican freedom fighters' find it impossible to successfully attack British military or police compounds in NI, as they have in the past.

So yesterday, out of mindless desperation, some narrow partisan group chose to kill innocent people…fellow Catholics and Protestants, fellow Irishmen, women and children, fellow nationalists and unionists who seek the same objectives albeit peacefully.

Patrick Pearse, the father of twentieth-century Irish republicanism, would not have bombed Omagh. Michael Collins, the man who won Ireland's War of Independence, would not have bombed Omagh. Gerry Adams, today's president of republican Sinn Fein would not have bombed Omagh and David Trimble, leader of the Ulster Unionist Party, would not have done so either. No, no one in his or her right mind would have staged that horrific assault on Omagh yesterday. So, please God, for all that is good and decent, it is time to stop the killings and punishment beatings on both sides of the political/sectarian divide. It is time to hasten the day when, as Yeats said, "...peace comes dropping slow, dropping from the veils of the morning to where the cricket sings...."

UNDER A BRILLIANT BLUE SKY...

UNDER A BRILLIANT
BLUE SKY...

For over a lifetime now, the Sunday closest to the 22nd of August has been a day of commemoration and remembrance in West Cork. Thousands of people from all over Ireland, yea even the world, arrive into a narrow bit of road running through the entrance of a subtle ravine, which meanders for some miles. Through this isolated slice of rural Irish countryside, about halfway between the towns of Macroom and Bandon in Co. Cork, is a spot called Bealnablath (pronounced: Bale/na/blah). The River Bride, a modest tributary, flows through and around lush fields and green vegetation, as it leisurely wends its way off toward the southwest. Popularly known as the Valley of Flowers, Bealnablath was the scene of the shortest but most significant battle in Irish history.

In the gathering gloom of evening on Tuesday, 22 August 1922, General Michael Collins was killed, murdered, maybe even assassinated, by a person or persons unknown. The controversy is unresolved to this day. Most tragically, the Big Fellow was the only person killed in a brief fire-fight, as members of his own Irish Free State army engaged a small contingent of Irish republican soldiers. These were some of the same men who had fought side-by-side with Collins for Ireland's independence only months before, but who now strongly opposed the treaty recently agreed to with England. (This political difference finally erupted into bitter civil war at the end of June, 1922 and would continue so until May, 1923.)

With the death of Collins, Ireland lost its greatest military and political leader of the twentieth century. (Tom Philbin, in his book *The Irish 100, A Ranking of the Most Influential Irish of All Time*, places Collins second, just behind St. Patrick, as having had the greatest impact on the Irish world.) So it is fitting that the people of Ireland should annually gather together at the spot where he died to pay tribute to this great leader and statesman.

The ceremony usually begins at three in the afternoon, but some begin arriving before noon. Parking is difficult on this narrow piece of road. Cars are strung out for a mile or more in either direction. Some park in nearby Crookstown and complete the journey by rented motor coach. More busloads of interested folk from other nearby towns converge as well, all adding to the growing congestion. The roadway passing Collins's memorial is finally closed to vehicular traffic at about one o'clock.

If the day is fair, people stand about in little knots talking in hushed voices. Others climb the grassy hill behind the white marble monument, hoping to find a comfortable spot from which to observe the ceremonies. Still more sit on the bank of the road or in open-doored cars, just waiting. A few can be seen walking up and down the road, talking and pointing. One can imagine they are retracing the movements of Collins's small, ill-fated military convoy, as they visualise the spots where ambush parties might have lain in wait.

If the day is wet, people wait inside their cars or join others in their vehicles, keeping dry and maybe having a bite of lunch or sharing a cup of tea. Some brave souls usually stand out under umbrellas before the large stone crucifix, talking while trying to keep their feet dry.

As the clock nears three, uniformed military and police personnel can be seen moving about. Martial music is heard in the distance. The band has arrived and is warming up. A lorry slowly makes its way through the crowd. The day's final props are offloaded. Folding chairs and a sound system are set up on the small raised platform surrounding the memorial. The Irish flag is raised then lowered to half-staff. The mass of onlookers begins to press forward in earnest. People near the back of the throng scramble to and fro, hoping to find better viewing positions.

Just before three, the invited dignitaries seem to appear from nowhere. Members of the Fine Gael political party, local politicians and other personalities take their seats on the dais. Finally, surviving members of the old Irish Republican Army (IRA), from its War of Independence days, are seated. They wear modest 1916 Easter Rebellion and/or War of Independence medal(s) proudly pinned to their jacket lapels. (Back in the 1960s and 1970s, there would be hundreds of the old guard in attendance. On my last Bealnablath Sunday in 1997 there were but two.)

The observance itself lasts only about an hour. The Irish national anthem is played and sung, a local priest offers prayers, celebrity introductions are made, ceremony organisers are recognised, the invited guest speaker pays tribute to Collins and to Ireland and, finally, "The Last Post" is played followed by a rifled salute.

Afterwards, people stand around chatting for a few minutes. Photographs are taken while some exchange addresses and telephone numbers. Others make arrangements to meet somewhere nearby and have a drink or something to eat. But within fifteen or twenty minutes, the crowd has moved off toward their waiting cars and coaches. Suddenly, the air is filled with the sound of hundreds of motor vehicles, all heading off up or down the road. Not a single blaring horn, however, is sounded.

By five that evening there is no one to be seen. The only remains of the afternoon tribute to Collins are the two or three wreaths left leaning against his monument. A few pieces of odd debris can be seen left lying on the ground. The small grassy area around the commemorative site is trampled and foot worn. Surprisingly though, few tire treads are visible in the muddy verge lining the road. As the afternoon shadows lengthen, Michael Collins's cenotaph is left to the quiet of another August Sunday evening. But rightfully so, the Big Fellow has left his indelible mark upon the Irish people. They will not soon forget this man who fought so gallantly for Ireland's freedom....

The following account was written for and published in the *Galway Advertiser* (Galway, Ireland) on Thursday, August 28, 1997. It was entitled "Under a brilliant blue sky." (On a sad note, the nephew of the Big Fellow mentioned below, also a Michael Collins, died in 2000. The Bealnablath Sunday ceremony will not be the same without him.)

A 1996 visit to West Cork and Michael Collins's family home site inspired me to write the poem *BEALNABLATH*.

❧

UNDER A BRILLIANT BLUE SKY...General Michael Collins(1890-1922), the first Chairman of Ireland's newly formed Free State Government, was honoured on Sunday last at Bealnablath, Co. Cork, the site at which he was ambushed and killed on 22 August 1922.

The annual roadside commemoration marking the 75th anniversary of Collins's death was attended by a larger than usual crowd of several thousand and featured a gathering of noted dignitaries. The overflow throng of loyal Irishmen and women was sprinkled with an assemblage of foreign visitors. Most of those present could be overheard discussing the details of the Big Fellow's controversial life and death. The names of filmmaker Neil Jordan and actor Liam Neeson were on many lips this year. They seemed to replace the usual references to Eamon de Valera and Arthur Griffith.

Under a brilliant blue sky and warm afternoon sun, those present heard Sean Donlon, former Irish ambassador to the United States, deliver an inspiring overview of Collins's many contributions which were so important to the shaping of modern-day Ireland. In addition, the noted career diplomat concluded his remarks with a thoughtful survey of the pending Belfast peace negotiations. He carefully pointed out that Collins was one of the first to recognise the principle of consent while ruling out unionist coercion as a means of overthrowing the governing power in the North.

Among the special guests were two aging invitees, Dan

O'Donovan of Tralee and Jack Kearney of Banteer, both original members of Co. Cork's old IRA Brigade. Also numerous noted politicos attended including former Fine Gael Taoiseach (Prime Minister) John Bruton and Justice Minister Nora Owen, MEP (Member, European Parliament) Mary Banotti, Dail (Irish parliament) members Paul Bradford, Austin Currie, Michael Finucane, Dan Neville, Jim O'Keefe and P.J. Sheehan. A handful of Co. Cork government officials plus some local luminaries also sat on the platform and later mingled with the crowd.

Finally, Michael Collins, Waterford Town nephew of the famous general, served as the event's Master of Ceremonies. In addition to shaking hands and talking with hundreds of old friends, he delivered an emotion-filled and touching tribute, on behalf of the entire Collins family, to those who had come to remember his gallant uncle.

Yes, the spirit of General Collins seemed to touch the hearts and souls of all those who made the trek to West Cork this day. They had all come to remember and honour one of Ireland's greatest heroes. They were also helping keep alive the spirit of those men and women who had fought and died over the centuries so Ireland might one day be free.

BEALNABLATH

It was in October long ago,
That a babe was born they say;
Who grew into a man renowned,
A legend in his day.
And as his love for Ireland bloomed,
He vowed he'd never stray;
Yet when he rode into Bealnablath,
His young life ebbed away.

From the Rising in the GPO,
With Connolly, Pearse and Clarke;
He came to feel a burning pride,
That imprisonment did further spark.
From his friendships formed in Frongoch Jail,
He groomed a band of men;
Collins urged them on and on,
Sure he'd not be a slave again.

His plots did foil the English lust,
To rule olde Eireann's land;
Their agent spies he did expose,
Deadly justice this Corkman's demand.
The bullets sped and death did rain,
And the Tans did burn the towns;
But young Collins wouldn't forsake his dream,
The Irish people he'd not let down.

Then the Sassenach cried, "We've had enough!"
And to London Mick did go;
A party of loyal Irishmen,
To sign a treaty so...
Olde Ireland would be free at last,
It was her ancient dream;
But as Collins hoped for a brand new day,
Once-loyal comrades had another scheme.

Sure, civil war poured out its awful death,
As hope for peace was lost;
While brothers fought and fathers died,
Olde Ireland paid the cost.
Though his pride burned strong, oh he strove to bend,
Yet his love was torn in two;
When Mick Collins returned to Bealnablath,
A fateful shot closed his eyes of blue.

No more would Collins dream of peace,
Nor have the strength to fight;
But his spirit lived in Ireland's heart,
As a republic sprang to life.
He had fought and died for Ireland's sake,
Like many a one before;
So when Mick Collins died at Bealnablath,
He'd be a hero forever more.

THE DAY HOPE
WAS BORN &
DIED...

THE DAY HOPE WAS
BORN & DIED...

This short, unpublished reminiscence speaks for itself. It was composed in August, 2000. The poem, *THE UNFORGOTTEN*, was written in the spring of 1994.

    THE DAY HOPE WAS BORN & DIED...Though long in the tooth, Ireland does not forget...at least not easily. Events of the far distant past still haunt the back streets of Eireann's memory. They emerge from the darkness at the odd moment. The 22nd of August is no exception.

    It was on that day in 'The Year of Liberty' (1798) that French General Jean Joseph Humbert landed on Irish soil at Killala Bay in Co. Mayo. With a thousand men, reinforced by hundreds of United Irishmen, Humbert went on the offensive. Marching his troops toward Castlebar, the French general caught the British Army by surprise, routing the Crown's forces. The resulting retreat became infamous. The 'Races of Castlebar' still fills many an Irish heart with justifiable pride. Unfortunately, once British Lord Charles Cornwallis and General Gerard Lake regained their balance, the tide turned in the other direction. Eventually outnumbered, the insurgents were soon crushed. Humbert surrendered to British government armed forces on 8 September. His French followers were treated as prisoners of war and were permitted to return home. The Irish officers, however, were court-martialled and hanged whilst their disarmed rebel followers were slaughtered... put to the sword. With Humbert's defeat, the United Irishmen's hope of a united, independent and non-sectarian Ireland was dashed to bits.

In 1922, one hundred and twenty-four years later, also on 22 August, the cause of Irish liberty was then riding on the shoulders of another general...this time an Irish one by the name of Michael Collins. Suddenly, Fate struck the Emerald Isle another cruel blow. As a small motorised column of Irish Free State soldiers entered the isolated, dusk-shrouded valley of Bealnablath in West Cork, rifle fire shattered the evening calm. A brief firefight ensued. Rebelling republican forces, who laid in wait for a chance to slay their former comrade and commander, pressed the attack for twenty minutes then re-treated.

It was the shortest and most costly battle in Irish history. Lying dead in the roadway was just one man, the Big Fellow himself. Collins, Commander-in-Chief of Ireland's recently established National Army, was only thirty-one years of age. His death eliminated any hope of a swift end to the fratricidal Civil War that now engulfed Ireland. A sniper's bullet ended any chance that the Corkman might work his magic again, bringing Ireland through another difficult time, as he had done during its recently concluded War of Independence. No, the fledging state would have to rely on others, men and women who lacked the insight, the charisma and the force of character possessed by Michael Collins. It would be a long time before the hatred and distrust that had spawned his death would be laid to rest.

So it is that the date of 22 August stands as one of the most singularly significant dates in Irish history. A date ripe with the prospect of hope and a date bitter with the tears of grief.

THE UNFORGOTTEN

Forever he had dreamed
A lifetime's journey.
Sure for years he had saved
Dollars tucked away;
Remembering his father's way of hiding
Some money each week,
Sent home for family and freedom;
The Famine's hard lesson.
He knelt down to pray.

All the cases were packed
Something tucked inside for each one.
Then the long ride to the airport
And his homeland but a dream;
Sunset and sunrise o'er the Atlantic
His restless legs longed to move,
But soon he'd be in Connemara;
The Famine remembered.
He bowed his head to pray.

The excitement of looking down on old Ireland's green
Wheels finally touching ground.
His uncle stood quietly and waited
With strong hands and a warm smile;
The question-filled ride home with so much to say
Surrounded by time for thoughtful silence,

Sloping sides of the Twelve Pins, waves on the bay;
The Famine rock ground.
He closed his eyes to pray.

Uncle lived alone in the family's thatched home
A warm fireside and a mantle of familiar faces.
By candlelight they sat talking of days 'fore and after
Old stories long forgotten, retold;
Visiting places and thinking over all the years
Some things seemed unchanged,
Even as new understanding grew;
The Famine still lives.
He clasped his hands to pray.

Alas, his time in the old homeland ended...
He repacked the cases.
Heavy-heartedness of leaving told in unspoken words
Wrapped time in silence;
He already missed this land of haunted smiles and silent
    tears
Forever pictured behind closed eyes,
Clouds blotted out the green and grey below;
Oh, the Famine would not die...
He crossed himself and prayed.

AT THE PICTURE HOUSE...

AT THE PICTURE HOUSE...

The following commentary regarding Neil Jordan's new film *Michael Collins* was written in September, 1996, after its Irish debut, and three weeks before its American opening on 11 October.

Today, the movie is available for rent or purchase on both DVD and VHS.

AT THE PICTURE HOUSE... The successful launch of Neil Jordan's film, *Michael Collins*, at the Venice (Italy) Film Festival last month has raised the hackles of a few critical bystanders for its glorification of Ireland's First Chairman of its Provisional Government, chosen in January, 1922, and (as historian T. Ryle Dwyer says) "the man who won the war." Once again, Collins faces the odious charge of being a terrorist (in Ireland's War of Independence, 1919-1921) whose life on film could upset the fragile peace process in Northern Ireland. (Ah sure, they must be joking!)

Of his newest effort, filmmaker Jordan (of *Interview with a Vampire* and *The Crying Game* fame) states, "I tried to make the Collins film as historically accurate as possible."

From a factual point-of-view, a student of Irish history could debate that point with Mr. Jordan, but for overall effect and for gaining a real feeling for the time, the filmmaker is spot on. His illustrations of the consequences of the uses of violence and its effects on a man who was desperately engaged in trying to pacify an ever-escalating situation are brilliant.

Some of Jordan's less myopic viewers will recognise that though Collins ordered the death of numerous spies and informers, innocent civilians never tasted his wrath. If that could only be said of Britain's infamous Black & Tans....

The film critic, Michael Sheridan, of the *Irish Independent*, recently commented on British attempts to vilify Jordan's so-called Irish republican hero.

> Other English papers...claimed Hollywood (Warner Brothers) was going to put a hold on a film that had any hint of succour for the IRA (Irish Republican Army). Past masters of film propaganda, the British were engaging in a dirty tricks campaign centred on the theory that the central character was a devil portrayed as a saint. Never mind that the British could blast the German Huns to hell in countless films, they were damned if they would let the Irish get away with the same thing.

Neil Jordan's *Michael Collins* opens in the States on October 11th. Go and judge for yourself....

SAY IT ISN'T SO...

SAY IT ISN'T SO...

On 1 January 2003, a story by Jill Lawless of *The Associated Press* grabbed headlines across the country as well as on the other side of the Atlantic. Ms. Lawless's surprising opening paragraph caught most people unaware. She stated that, "At the height of bloodletting in Northern Ireland, the British government considered trying to end the sectarian conflict by forcibly moving hundreds of thousands of Catholics to the Irish Republic, according to records released Wednesday."

The following is a reply to this revelation. It appeared in the 19 March 2003 issue of *The Irish Echo* (New York City).

SAY IT ISN'T SO (British government duplicity)...Is it any wonder why Irish republicans, those seeking a 32-county united Ireland, have reason to mistrust the British government and their loyalist collaborators, those determined to maintain Northern Ireland's ties with England? *The Associated Press* report of today entitled, "1972 paper reveals Britain considered ethnic cleansing," just scratches the surface regarding the British government's 'dirty tricks' of a generation ago. To think that Westminster's leadership would even consider forcibly uprooting thousands of Irish Catholics living in Northern Ireland (NI), and moving them to the Republic or placing them "...into homogenous enclaves within Northern Ireland..." is a dastardly plot born of unscrupulous politicians.

The sectarian violence and hatred spawned in NI, begun in the late 1960s, was a direct result of Britain's failure to control the loyalist Protestant powerbrokers living in the Six Counties. This political and economic leadership, along with their followers, were unwilling to grant any fair measure of democratic peace with justice to their Catholic neighbours.

Equal housing, fair employment, voting rights, British-promised civil-liberty reforms were some of the demands NI Catholics sought via non-violent avenues. The British government, British army and NI loyalist sympathisers refused to bargain or to grant these essential democratic requests. As a result, peaceful demonstrations turned ugly.

Britain's chequered and pockmarked treatment of its Northern Irish Catholic citizenry is appalling. Internment without trial, Diplock courts (trials without juries), suspension of habeas corpus, police and British military complicity in illegal acts against people and property are but a few of the injustices spawned in the Six Counties during the last third of the twentieth century. Now, this disclosure of an ethnic cleansing scheme paints an even sadder story of law and order gone terribly wrong.

Today, distrust of British and unionist government policies and their promises raises more questions and apprehensions than it answers.

A TRILL TRIO
FROM AMERICA...

A TRILL TRIO FROM
AMERICA...

To no one's surprise, Northern Ireland's (NI) newly devolved government lurched along amid many fits and starts. Everybody knew it would not be easy. Consequently, the architects of the Good Friday Peace Accord, anticipating setbacks, unforeseen snags and inevitable delays, built into its launch timetable an eighteen-month implementation window. Planners foresaw the predictable teething troubles individuals might have working together harmoniously. An Agreement referendum, assembly elections, formation of a shadow executive plus the organising of all the particulars required to set up a supportive governmental administration required time. Additionally, the Agreement obligated the Irish people to amend their 1937 constitution, giving up all claims to the Six Counties, while the British government needed to rescind its 1920 Government of Ireland Act that partitioned Ireland.

When the executive met for the first time on 1 July 1998, David Trimble, leader of the dominant Protestant Ulster Unionist Party, was chosen First Minister designate of the Assembly. Seamus Mallon, number two man in the leading Catholic/nationalist Social Democratic and Labour Party, was selected Deputy First Minister designate. After a few other formalities, the body adjourned. There was much behind-the-scenes work to be done.

Early that autumn, two months after the Omagh bombing and Gerry Adams's statement that violence in the North must end, an historic meeting took place. On 10 September 1998, Adams, the consummate republican, and David Trimble, the epitome of unionism, met and talked. It was the first time such a meeting had been held

179

since the 1922 talks between Michael Collins, chairman of the Provisional government of the recently created Irish Free State, and James Craig, prime minister of the new Northern Irish satellite state. The encounter, another dividend of the Good Friday Accord, produced little, as was the case with the Collins-Craig confab years before, but at least the two leaders had started a dialogue.

The major stumbling block, at least in Trimble's mind, was the apparent unresponsive attitude of the IRA regarding the decommissioning of its weapons. The Agreement, intentionally vague on this argumentative point to permit some negotiating leeway, suggested all parties with ties to paramilitaries had two years, until 22 May 2000, to hand in their illegal arms. Trimble was in a hurry. Adams was not. Both men were posturing while not wanting to concede something without a satisfactory quid pro quo.

The Agreement stated that a 'shadow' power-sharing executive be chosen by the end of October, 1998 and functioning by February, 1999. In reality, it would be this body of twelve individuals, chosen by the 108-person Assembly from the dominant Northern Irish political parties that would make most of the decisions regarding the governance of the Six Counties. But resolving matters and making decisions took much longer than was hoped. Creating governmental departments and selecting ministers to head them as well as establishing cross-border bodies was a slow process. Predictably, however, the most difficult task of all was forming an executive composed of past political and ideological adversaries: men and women who did not like, much less trust, one another. Setting aside political differences and fostering confidence among former 'enemies' is never an easy matter, especially in NI.

Paradoxically, the Belfast Accord reversed the traditional political roles in the North. Now, it was the unionists' turn to give and the nationalists' turn to take. Unfortunately, this latter group was unaccustomed to being on the receiving end of the process.

Finally, on the first of December, 1999 the full Assembly, with its new executive in place, met for the first time. At long last, Westminster had transferred back the power to govern the people of Northern Ireland to the fledgling Belfast Assembly.

One can only wonder, if things had been different down through the years, what the Six Counties might be like today. Over time, the bitterness of sectarianism and distrust had destroyed so much of NI's political and economic potential and arrested its natural cultural and social evolution.

Three other significant spin-offs of the Belfast Accord should also be noted. On 2 December 1999 the Republic of Ireland formally relinquished its constitutional claim to the Six Counties. Secondly, the British government repealed the Government of Ireland Act of 1920. That legislation, a rejoinder to the 1916 Easter Rebellion, had partitioned Ireland, creating the contentious dependency. With the revocation of those two statutes, the fate of Northern Ireland now rested in the hands of its new government and upon the collective wishes of its newly empowered citizens. Finally, on 18 December 1999, the Loyalist Volunteer Force, a Protestant paramilitary organisation, turned in a small cache of illegally held weapons. This was the first time such a group had done so in all the storied annals of Irish revolutionary history.

The following three short commentaries were written during the summer of 1999. They express my apprehension and irritation regarding the slow evolution of Northern Ireland's devolved government. Two of the statements appeared in the *Irish Echo* (New York City) and one in *The Cincinnati Enquirer* (Cincinnati, Ohio).

ADAMS SHOULD PLAY THE GREEN CARD NOW...

Don't let Northern Ireland's political/peace process die. By folding our hand now, Ulster unionism's bloody-mindedness crawls away with an undeserved victory wrapped in their own 'orange' political self-interests. History tells us violence can not win the day any longer. There are too many guns and not enough blood. Nobody wins that war...everyone loses.

Instead, nationalists and republicans should unite and play our 'green' card. Don't chuck it away now when the odds are in our favour. The Irish people, both north and south, overwhelmingly want peace and reform. Political prisoners are being repatriated and freed. Devolved internal and cross-border governmental bodies are poised for action. Money has been allocated and waits spending. The Royal Ulster Constabulary (NI's police force) is undergoing close examination for its questionable practices. The British army is pulling back. Those responsible for Bloody Sunday, Pat Finucane's murder and more are under the public's microscope for the first time ever. Positive changes are in the wind. A reunited Ireland finally might just be in sight.

No, not everything is perfect, but the machinery is in gear to deliver a peace with more justice than the guns have wrought. Now is the time to call the unionists' bluff. Lead by example: champion a measured decommissioning timetable. Let the political process and public opinion work for us instead of against us. Let all Irishmen and women be the beneficiaries of positive change in Northern Ireland. (May, 1999)

TRIMBLE'S RESPONSIBILITY FOR DEVOLVED GOVERNMENT...

The outrage and disbelief of the recent debacle at Parliament Buildings in Belfast slowly retreats toward mind-boggling disappointment. Northern Ireland's seventeen-month-old odyssey toward a devolved government with a power-sharing executive, teetering so long on razor's edge, has collapsed, slicing itself to bits. Brazenly and with great recklessness, the dogmatic unionists, led by David Trimble, have defied the will of the electorate (71% in Northern Ireland and 94% in the Irish Republic). They have refused to follow through on implementing the terms of the Good Friday Peace Accord that all major political parties agreed to in April, 1998.

Mr. Trimble states, "No guns, no Government," but the terms of that signed agreement maintain, "Government first, guns decommissioned by May, 2000." So, by refusing to empanel an executive composed of unionists, nationalists and republicans, Trimble has broken his word. He has denied the people of the North the justice they want and so rightly deserve.

Clearly, the Ulster Unionist Party (UUP) is unwilling to acknowledge that a transformation in thinking has occurred in Ireland. Guns and violence are no longer seen as the medium through which political power is gained. For the most part, the major paramilitary groups have upheld their cease-fires and have turned to the negotiating table for discussions. But, unfortunately, the North is so pockmarked with failure and mistrust that mutual respect is virtually unknown. Coupled with this is the unionists' fear they will be swallowed up by the rising tide of public opinion, springing from the dream, the hope, and the promise of a lasting peace with justice. Clearly, the UUP does not represent the majority of its constituents or know how to move forward in positive meaningful ways.

If Mr. Trimble is truly a man of peace (1998 Nobel

peace prize co-winner) rather than just another egotistical political opportunist, he must change tactics without delay. He must help birth a long-denied, devolved government in Belfast. (July, 1999)

WHAT PRICE PEACE?...

I am sick of the violence in Northern Ireland and tired of the one-sided reporting about it in the American press (Re: *The New York Times*, 15 August 1999, "Protests turn violent in Northern Ireland"). The entire tone of this story was most certainly biased, inflammatory and anti-Catholic.

Now, do not think for one moment I am condoning or endorsing the use of violence in Northern Ireland, but the repeated newspaper reference to the 'IRA this and Catholics that' all too often misinforms. Yes, the Irish Republican Army and its splinter groups have been guilty of gross atrocities in support of their cause of uniting Ireland and freeing it of British rule, but this is only half the story. There are just as many determined loyalists in Northern Ireland who are bent on seeing their ill-gotten power base maintained and their flagging union with Britain preserved.

Irish history is liberally sprinkled with loyalist paramilitary groups who have murdered, terrorised, threatened and destroyed the lives and property of Irish and British citizens alike. Each of these groups is often tied directly or indirectly to unionist political machinery or influential pressure groups. Fully half the deaths in the North during the last thirty years are their responsibility, but where are the reports about how loyalists are *not* decommissioning their illegally held weapons? Little is reported regarding how unionists are undermining efforts to establish a devolved northern government...a government charged by the vast majority of the people with promoting a lasting peace with justice in Northern Ireland. (August, 1999)

THE BEST OF OLDE
GALWAY TOWN...

THE BEST OF OLDE
GALWAY TOWN...

One evening several years ago, when I was feeling particularly nostalgic for Ireland, I sat down at my typewriter. Yes, I still had one of those contraptions back then, and wrote the following for my own pleasure. Entitled 'Grand Olde Galway Town,' I reminisced about the times I led tours around the city in an old 1963 Leland double-decked, open-topped bus. (Thanks be to God, I was the one with the microphone in my hand and not the steering wheel.) To this musing, I added a short piece written back in 1993 on the occasion of that year's oyster festival.

This charming celebration was founded in 1954 and, with the sponsorship support of Guinness, has become one of Ireland's most enjoyable yearly events. Besides the pints and oysters, the town is filled with music, song, family entertainment and lots of people just having a good time of it. That year American comedian Bob Hope and his wife were Galway's special guests. To the delight of the assembled throng, the honoured couple led the traditional, folksy oyster parade through the streets of the old town.

I wrote the poem *THE OLD MAN OF GALWAY* one winter's night in 1994.

THE BEST OF OLDE GALWAY TOWN…As familial urges cry out pulling Americans back to their ancestral homelands, as economic good fortune increases many a person's disposable income, as one's wanderlust and frequent-flyer mileage proliferate, countless millions of holiday seekers from this side of the Atlantic continue to head eastward toward Europe and beyond.

Lately, one of the most popular destinations for the distributors of the Yankee dollar is Ireland, the land of green hills, ancient castles and a slower, gentler way of life. The Irish are famous for welcoming strangers into their midst. Their friendly smiles, love of music and storytelling plus their warm hospitality are often the highlight of many a sightseer's holiday. And now, with the promise of peace in Northern Ireland, even more travellers are bent on sampling the best of historic, storied Ireland.

Having recently returned to America from the 'Land of the Gaels,' I thought I would try and whet your appetite, inviting you to sample one of Ireland's oldest and finest cities, Galway.

Located on the western side of the 'Island of Saints and Scholars,' Gaillimh, the Town of Foreigners, is a delightful mix of old and new. It was founded by the Anglo-Norman conqueror, Richard De Burgo in 1232. The soon-to-be-thriving city-state, located on the River Galvia (now River Corrib) and nestled beside beautiful Galway Bay, became a major old-world trading port in the 15th, 16th and 17th centuries.

Unfortunately, the vicissitudes of wealth and war eventually diminished its importance. Soon Galwegians would languish under the lash of England and later the British Empire. Sure religious persecution, famine, emigration and economic hardship all took their toll.

Happily, with Irish independence firmly established in twenty-six of its thirty-two counties, Ireland and Galway's fortunes turned around in the second half of the twentieth century. Today, the City of Tribes boasts over 60,000 inhabitants and a bustling economy. It is one of the fastest growing cities in Western Europe.

While new construction is very much in evidence, Galway's reverence and love of its grand and glorious past is nobly preserved. Many centuries-old buildings remain for all the world to see and celebrate.

So if the cities of Dublin, Cork or Belfast are your only memories of Ireland, I invite you to mark your calendar for the last weekend in September. That is when Galway hosts its famous Oyster Festival. Once again, with the summer's tourists safely back home, the old city is given back to the Irish and the Galwegians for their own pleasure and enjoyment. Ah sure, there are the odd stragglers left over from a summer filled with Bacchanalian pursuits, but for the most part, it is the 'locals' who are left to entertain each other and you.

From the traditional, quaint and folksy parade down Shop Street led by an aged, shawl-bedecked Claddagh woman carrying a simple handwoven reed basket filled with seaweed and barnacle-encrusted Galway Bay oysters, to the pubs that overflow with Irish music, laughter, storytelling and refreshing libations, these special three days are not to be missed. Aye and be assured that the Irish salmon, homemade chowder, freshly baked brown bread and Ireland's traditional black stout never tastes any grander.

Then while the last of the warm autumn sun flushes skyward-turned faces, a walk along Salthill's promenade, bordering Galway Bay, brings thoughts of yesterday and recollections of famine-filled coffin ships. Lingering echoes of lost yesterdays mingle gently with the hopes of a new tomorrow.

Almost imperceptibly, as the sea breeze quickens and the sound of music swells inside you like the incoming tide, your sentimental Irish soul realises it has returned again home...home from across the sea....

THE OLD MAN OF GALWAY

The rush of the Corrib as it pours out to sea,
Reminds him of a time when his dreams were so free.
He'd hoped and he'd prayed for a life of his own,
But the famine and landlord had demanded his home.
Now he walks with no swagger as the wind blows cold,
He is really quite young, yet he looks oh so old.
Haggard and sad-faced, he drinks all alone,
Sits quietly and dreams of his forsaken home.

Does he sing his song slowly?
Does he play its chords lowly?
Does he hide in the shadows of a youth that's grown
    old?
Does your man play the banjo and dream all alone?
Sure his heart it grows sad in his troubled land.

Now he pushes his chair back and rises to go,
But pausing he looks toward the fire's warm glow.
Ah sure, sad memories wash over him then,
So he sits back down and he orders again.
Quietly, deeply and always he drinks,
To drown out the sorrows and ghosts that he thinks...
Haunt him and curse him, his life so alone,
Will he ever find caring and a love of his own?

Does he sing the song slowly?
Does he play its chords lowly?
Does he hide in the shadows of a youth that's grown
    cold?
Do you play the banjo and dream all alone?
Does your heart grow sad for this tortured man?

With each new day's dawning, no hope does he know,
So it's back to the pub, where else can he go?
 The black creamy foam of his loved Irish stout,
And the sharp, sweet taste of cheap whiskey call out.
Oh the rain, oh the rain, oh it's wet everywhere,
With the wind blowing hard there's no reason to care.
As the old man of Galway fades from our view,
Will we hurry through life; will we be like him too?

Do you sing your song slowly?
Do you play its chords lowly?
Do you hide in the shadows of your youth that's grown
   old?
Do you play your banjo and dream all alone?
Does your heart grow sad in the Stranger's land?

THATCHER'S
VOICE
SILENCED...

THATCHER'S VOICE
SILENCED...

As much as I promised myself I would not beat the Lambeg drum for Margaret Thatcher's eleven-year reign over Northern Ireland in the 1980s, I could not resist. Book after book has been written about her role in Northern Irish political life. Depending on your point of view, she was either a great stateswoman or the evil-doing 'Iron Lady.' I certainly give Ms. Thatcher credit for the inspired leadership model she provided other women in the world of politics traditionally dominated by men. But I can not agree with or abide by her attitude, policies and treatment of Northern Ireland and its minority Catholic/nationalist/republican population.

At the end of March, 2002, I was surprised to read Philip Terzian's editorial about Ms. Thatcher. Mr. Terzian is the associate editor of the *Providence Journal* and his syndicated columns appear in a great many newspapers throughout the United States.

The particular column that I refer to above was entitled, "Margaret Thatcher, Voice silent, ideas heeded." In this editorial, Mr. Terzian notes that the seventy-seven-year-old former British Prime Minister has had a "series of small strokes," leaving her unable to speak in public. The associate editor goes on to say that though Ms. Thatcher remains cool toward Britain's involvement with the European Union, Europe's feelings toward her have warmed. Maybe attitudes have changed out of nostalgic sentimentality for the aging politician or maybe it is because she has not been in office to meddle in the affairs of their "...classic centrally planned socialist state..." for the past dozen years. Who knows?

Terzian points out that it was her policies in the 1980s that "...made possible the rise of Tony Blair..." and Britain's modern

Labour Party. The writer also notes that the lessons of Thatcherism are alive and well in the States. He points out, "While the Bush administration is distracted by the war on terrorism, Democrats in congress have been pushing to strengthen, not loosen, the government's regulatory powers and frustrate efforts to liberalize markets." Who can forget Ms. Thatcher's role in tackling British labour unions, privatising public industries and her inflexible attitude regarding Northern Ireland?

The following reply, written on 1 April 2002 (and this is no joke), rebuts Mr. Terzian's image of Margaret Thatcher.

THATCHER'S VOICE SILENCED...I have followed Margaret Thatcher's career with great interest, as have many Irish as well as others. I am sorry for her physical 'troubles,' but take no comfort in her political legacy.

Philip Terzian, in his recent tribute to the former British prime minister, paints Ms. Thatcher in the likeness of a demi-saint: a political, economic and social reformer par excellence. I doubt Mr. Terzian ever lived in a Welsh colliery town or on a Belfast back street during the 1970s or 1980s. If he had, I wonder if he would have waxed so eloquently about the 'Iron Lady.' As British Prime Minister from 1979 to 1990, Ms. Thatcher's chequered career was pockmarked with limiting individual and group civil liberties while often opposing the fostering of democratic ideals.

As a responsible leader, she and her government did little to resolve the complex issues they inherited in Northern Ireland. Her reaction to the eleven-month, multi-party Irish Freedom Forum in 1984 is legend. She made the three-letter word 'OUT' sound like a four-letter expletive. Thatcher's attitude toward Irish prisoners on hunger strike in 1981 was tantamount to murder. Her administration's passage of the Northern Irish Emergency Provisions Act and the Prevention of Terrorism Act in the late 1980s provided radical and harsh measures that curbed individual freedoms and legally injected the power of 'Big Brother' into the lives of anyone the authorities chose.

Under her reign, the British government spent millions of dollars in the United States fighting the MacBride Principles, designed to support Catholic equal-employment opportunities in the Six Counties. Many of her foreign policies favoured apartheid which supported discrimination in South Africa. Sadly, this is but a partial list.

According to a Reuter's story written by David Storey in 1992, "In her eleven-year rule, Thatcher emasculated the powerful trade unions, privatised state industries and promoted individual liberty over social responsibility."

Much of Margaret Thatcher's political record deserves to be silenced, but not forgotten. May it serve as an enduring example to future generations that might be tempted to replicate Britain's calamitous track record of colonial imperialism over the centuries.

NOBODY SAID IT WOULD BE EASY...

NOBODY SAID IT WOULD
BE EASY...

The year 2000 was marked by progress and backsliding. In January, Northern Irish Secretary Peter Mandelson initiated legislation reforming the North's police force. The semi-military Royal Ulster Constabulary's (RUC) days were numbered. The Police Service of Northern Ireland (PSNI), hopefully a more diverse and democratic institution, was being organised, another dividend of the Belfast Agreement. This had been one of the nationalists' principal demands. The ranks of the RUC were more than ninety percent Protestant, and complaints of discrimination and underhandedness were issues the Catholic population in the Six Counties had continuously voiced.

In February, a crisis occurred. London was forced to impose direct rule over the affairs of the Northern Irish people. It did so in order to avoid the collapse of the new coalition government. This cooling-off period allowed its newly elected officials to remain in office while fresh negotiations were undertaken in Belfast. Once again, David Trimble, flexing his unionist muscles, had forced the issue over lack of republican army decommissioning.

The matter had actually come to a head back at the end of 1999, with the October delay regarding the announcement of ministerial department assignments and cross-border bodies' allocations. United States Senator George Mitchell, chosen by President Clinton to broker the Good Friday Agreement in 1998, returned to NI to help break the deadlock resulting over the timing of arms decommissioning. The diplomat's deal was simple. Trimble's party, the Ulster Unionists, would drop their demand for immediate IRA disarmament prior to the Protestant-Catholic coalition cabinet's formation, on the condition that the IRA begin prompt disposal of its weapons *prior* to the May, 2000 mandate. As part of the original Agreement, an independent decommissioning body would supervise and verify all arms destruction.

In January, however, the disarmament commission filed a negative report. Trimble threatened to bring down the devolved government if the British did not act. Rather than dissolve the executive, forcing new elections, London acted by suspending the eight-week-old assembly. (This behaviour by Trimble of either threatening to resign his position as executive leader or forcing Britain to suspend the government was to become a common practice in the months ahead.)

Sinn Fein's reaction was predictable. Gerry Adams stated that the IRA would not disarm under those conditions. He called the Ulster Unionist leader's handling of the situation "a disaster."

In defence of Trimble's actions, it must be pointed out that he was under great pressure from his own party membership. His role as their leader was under attack. An anti-agreement faction within the Ulster Unionist Party was growing more resonant, demanding additional concessions from the nationalists and republicans. Many doubts and suspicions surfaced as the ultra-unionists faced the reality of sharing power with their republican 'enemy.'

On the other hand, Gerry Adams had a heavy burden to bear as well. Elements within Sinn Fein balked at being told what to do by unionists, their time-honoured foe. The historical tradition of the gun in Irish politics does not die easily. Faced with the danger of another possible republican split that could have dire consequences for everyone, Adams walked a perilous path.

The drama ended in May. On the 6th, the IRA announced its commitment to put its arms 'completely and verifiably' beyond use, as per the terms of the Good Friday Accord. The British government, keeping its word, restored devolved powers to the Belfast government at month's end. The crisis was over, at least for now.

In June the IRA made an historic move. It announced the opening of arms dumps to the international independent decommissioning body. Things were back on track once more.

In July, the mood in the North changed again. News reports painted a bleak picture as anti-Catholic extremists again threatened the streets of Northern Ireland with their annual Orange Order marches. Police and British army soldiers, along with countless civilians, prepared for 'war,' if the Protestant fraternal group was not allowed to conduct a banned march through the main Catholic district of Portadown, Co. Armagh. The threats of recently re-incarcerated Johnny 'Mad Dog' Adair, who bragged that he killed over one hundred Catholic civilians in his life, attested to the fact that sectarianism was alive and well in the Six Counties. Good Friday Agreement or not, hatred and bigotry continued to be an ingrained way of life in Northern Ireland.

Finally, two other positive dividends of the peace process are worthy of note. At the end of July, the last of the Maze 'political' prisoners were released from incarceration. A total of 428 men and women from both communities had been freed on condition of good behaviour. (Adair was one of those men, but because of parole violations, he was later rearrested in 2002.)

The year ended, as 1995 had, with a visit to Dublin and Belfast by out-going American President Bill Clinton. He had come to reap the fruits of his efforts that helped bring peace to the island of Ireland and a new government to the North.

The following are three short essays written in 2000, expressing my reactions to the year's happenings. The first two appeared in the *Irish Echo*, the largest Irish-American newspaper published in New York City.

NOW IS TIME TO FIND COMMON GROUND IN NORTH...

Recent reports from the North paint Gerry Adams and Sinn Fein as the bad guys and David Trimble and his Ulster Unionists as maintaining the high moral ground.

From the outside looking in, it seems so simple: the IRA decommissions its weapons and all will be right in Northern Ireland.

But history teaches hard lessons, especially to those who refuse to learn from them. For more than eight hundred and fifty years England/Great Britain selfishly dominated Irish affairs. Levels of distrust, dislike, resentment, even hatred ran deeply on both sides. The old imperial ploy of divide-and-conquer is not easily forgotten. Today, both nationalist/republicans and unionist/loyalists do not want to appear weak or powerless for fear of losing face...the 'no surrender' syndrome. Self-interests quickly bubble up blotting out the common good. Trimble decreed a 31 January deadline for 'significant' paramilitary disarmament to commence or his party would withdraw from the North's new government. Gerry Adams fears if the IRA is forced to capitulate before the Good Friday Agreement's May 2000 deadline, it might precipitate a split in republican solidarity, leading to a renewal of military violence. For the present, some hard-liners think just keeping their guns silent is a significant concession, showing their sincere commitment to peace.

Northern Ireland politics is a dangerous tightrope with life and death consequences for all concerned. Self-interests should not blot out the last twenty-two months of peaceful progress and budding good will. Now is the time for another 'Camp David' miracle with Washington, London and Dublin working with Northern Irish politicos in finding some common ground so all may proudly stand tall. The guns will cease to be a stumbling block when peace is allowed to grow and blossom. (March, 2000)

QUESTION TO TRIMBLE: STATUS QUO
OR REFORM?...

Selfless or selfish? At first glance, it appears there is reason to celebrate. Catholics and Protestants, nationalists and unionists, republicans and loyalists have agreed, again, to share power and work together under the guise of a devolved, home-ruled government in Northern Ireland (NI). But history has a way of continually casting a dark shadow over the Emerald Isle. Once more, the warning words of David Trimble, the Ulster Unionists' leader, bear watching: "It is obvious there are limits to how much more we can be stretched."

With party support dwindling, 71% in May, 1998, 57% this February and 53% last month, his political-power and voice-of-moderation days may be numbered. The question is: will Trimble continue fighting for what is right in Northern Ireland ...peace with justice for all, or will he bow to the traditionalists in order to save his political skin?

Assuming the Irish Republican Army follows through with its pledge of putting its weapons beyond use, Trimble faces the unpleasant task of spearheading his dominant party's restructuring of Northern Ireland's myopic police force. Hopefully, this Nobel peace prize winner will place the interests of all NI on the table and push for Royal Ulster Constabulary reform rather than merely seeking to consolidate his own political base and settling for the status quo.

If he does not, the newly redevolved NI government will likely fail and the hope of a lasting peace in Ireland will continue to be a nightmare instead of a dream come true. (June, 2000)

PEACE WITH JUSTICE...

If ye seek peace, tread first the path of justice...peace will follow.

In its quest for both, Northern Ireland convulses once again as the anniversary of King William III's victory over King James II at the 1690 Battle of the Boyne draws nigh (12 July). Echoing a sadly familiar ring, extremists posture, threatening to disrupt the tenuous 'peace with justice' carefully being nursed to life in Ulster's Six Counties.

Back in the 1950s and early 1960s, before Catholic nationalists posed a political threat to Protestant unionist domination, the summer 'marching season' was something to be tolerated, even ignored. But during the 1970s and 1980s, with the rise of civil right demands and Irish republicans standing up to loyalist ruffians, the Orange Order marches became contentious and violent.

Now, with the century-old power base shifting toward a middle ground, die-hard unionists, loyal only unto themselves, refuse to acknowledge the changes demanded of them by the majority of their brethren. Today and for weeks to come thousands of Ulster Unionist and Orangemen will don their sashes and bowler hats in blatant disregard for the rights and well-being of others. Their annual parades, many through Catholic neighbourhoods, strike fear, arouse anger and are a public embarrassment. These ceremonial displays are simply acts of triumphalism aimed at demeaning, degrading and denigrating Catholics while abashing much of their own Protestant community. As Johnny 'Mad Dog' Adair, a key Ulster Freedom Fighter terrorist, again threatens Portadown Catholics with violence, may justice win out and peace prevail.

The past dies hard in Ireland, but this horrific chapter must be brought to a close. Its shadow cannot be permitted to blight the bright, new dawn now breaking o'er Ireland. (July, 2000)

JOHN PATTON EMMET REVISITED...

JOHN PATTEN EMMET

REMEMBERED...

Even today, the family name of Emmet strikes a chord in the heart of nearly every Irish person. Most remember Robert Emmet's stirring speech from the dock prior to his brutal execution on 20 September 1803 in Dublin's Thomas Street. The British authorities had hoped to quash any ideas about further rebellion after Emmet's short-lived revolt that July.

The great poetic Irish writer Thomas Moore often surreptitiously honoured his friend's death in verse. Songs such as "The Minstrel Boy," "Lay His Sword By His Side" and, especially, "O Breathe Not His Name" were written in Emmet's memory. The latter one refers to the words attributed to the condemned Emmet, "When my country takes her place among the nations of the earth, then and not till then, let my epitaph be written."

Robert's brother, Thomas Addis Emmet (John Patten's father), was also a noted patriot and lawyer. In fact, there were several Emmets who made lasting contributions to the cause of Ireland over the years. John Patten Emmet nobly carried on the family tradition.

The following piece, written in 1997, was intended to enlighten others as to the man's greatness. The poem, *'TIS IRELAND, MY FREELAND,* was penned in 1995.

JOHN PATTEN EMMET REMEMBERED... Recently, while visiting the university town of Charlottesville, Virginia (pop. 45,000), I discovered a special link with Ireland. Not surprisingly, the home of America's third president, Thomas Jefferson, has strong Irish connexions. He employed many Irish craftsmen to help build his home, Monticello, and his newly founded University of Virginia.

There is more, however, to this Jefferson-Irish link. Just a short stroll up Sprigg Lane, only 150 yards west of Emmet Street, brings the curiosity seeker to number 209-211, Morea House. Before you stands a fine nineteenth-century vernacular brick building surrounded by aged trees and simple gardens. This was the home of John Patten Emmet (1796-1842). He was the University of Virginia's first professor of natural history, and later, the honouree of one of Charlottesville's main thoroughfares.

While a man of renown in his transplanted America, it should be noted that other members of Emmet's Irish family also adorn history's pages. Dr. John P. Emmet, born in Dublin on 8 April 1796, was the second son of famous lawyer and United Irishman, Thomas Addis Emmet (1764-1827). Furthermore, Thomas's brother and John's uncle was none other than Robert Emmet (1778-1803) himself.

It was Robert, another United Irishman, who led the infamous Dublin Rising of 23 July 1803. Two months later, he was half-hanged, drawn, quartered and beheaded by the British authorities for his traitorous actions. Ironically, John's grandfather was the highly respected Dr. Robert Emmet, whose patient responsibilities included Ireland's Lord Lieutenant, England's official representative to their island neighbour, during the late eighteenth century.

John's father, Thomas, was imprisoned in Scotland during March, 1798 for his anti-English political activities in Ireland just prior to the outbreak of fighting spawned by the Rising of '98. The failed rebellion saw more than 30,000 put to England's sword in that savage summer and autumn's 'Year of Liberty.' After spending four years behind bars, Thomas was released in 1802. From Scotland, he moved to Paris and finally, with his family in tow, immigrated to America in 1804. It was in New York City that Thomas's legal practice flourished, as he often represented a growing and needy Irish immigrant population.

During his early years in the United States, John Patten Emmet received a classical education at a Long Island academy. After graduation, he enrolled in the United States Military Academy at West Point, New York. His growing reputation as a mathematician earned him a position on the faculty while still pursuing his undergraduate degree.

In 1817, John's continued poor health forced him to leave school. He spent most of the next two years in Italy studying music, sculpture and painting. Returning to New York in 1819, John entered medical school and was graduated in 1822.

After practicing medicine for three years in Charleston, South Carolina, Dr. Emmet accepted the chair of Professor of Natural History at the newly established University of Virginia in Charlottesville. At the young age of 29, his expanding reputation as a chemist and inventor had attracted the attention of Thomas Jefferson.

As a bachelor, Emmet lived in Pavilion I on the West Lawn of the University. There he lectured on a wide range of subjects including zoology, botany, mineralogy, chemistry, geology and rural economy. Dr. Emmet's teaching skills were highly respected and his lectures were attended by students and fellow professors as well as curious townspeople.

In 1827, the Board of Visitors (appointed university overseers) lightened his teaching load. He now concentrated his energies on being strictly a Professor of Chemistry and Materia Medica. During that same year, he married Mary Byrd Tucker, daughter of a prominent and wealthy Virginia family. In time, they became the proud parents of three children.

In 1831, John Patten Emmet purchased a one-hundred-six-acre farm bordered on one side by what is now Sprigg Lane, and three years later began building Morea House. No definite documentation exists to verify that Emmet designed the house, but from his reputation as an inventor and skilled draftsman, it seems very likely that he authored or at least helped design the plans for his new home.

Completed one year later, in 1835 at a cost of $2,500, the two-and-a-half-story brick structure incorporated many Jeffersonian architectural features. Located only a short distance from the University's Academic Village, it is the only surviving structure built by an original faculty member.

Emmet had bought the acreage to pursue his hobbies of silk making, horticulture and wine production. The name Morea was taken from the botanical name of the Chinese mulberry tree, *Morus multicaulis*, whose leaves form the staple diet of the silkworm. The shadows of some of these original trees still grace the now two-and-a-half-acre property. Additionally, several offshoots from tree saplings brought back to Jefferson by Lewis and Clark from their great 1804-1806 expedition to the Northwest were transplanted on Emmet's property. They may still be seen growing on the grounds today.

It is widely accepted that because of its close proximity to the University, Dr. Emmet probably conducted many of his subsequent lectures from inside Morea's handsome walls. Quite possibly, he also held classes on its spacious lawns during Virginia's warm summer months.

The Doctor enjoyed only seven years of residence at Morea House. He died suddenly on 15 August 1842 while on a journey from Charleston to New York. That autumn, his fellow faculty members paid him special tribute for his seventeen years of distinguished service to the University, the community and the world of science and learning. At the age of forty-six, he was buried at Marble Cemetery in New York City.

Unfortunately, his wife died just three years later with the house passing from Emmet family hands in 1847. It was rumoured that Dr. William Holmes McGuffey, author of the famous *The Eclectic First Reader for Children with Pictures*, 'took his meals at Morea,' while the building served as a boarding house after the Emmets sold it. Today, the University of Virginia owns the dwelling.

John Patton Emmet's first child, born in Charlottesville, quite possibly on the family's kitchen table in Pavilion I, became the third family member to be named Thomas Addis Emmet (1829-1919). This younger Dr. Emmet, following in his family's footsteps, became a noted physician, lawyer and writer. Among his written efforts were a detailed family history and a comprehensive volume on Irish immigration. A personalised copy of this book still resides at the University.

As a postscript, John Patton Emmet's son, the third Thomas, spent the later years of his life tracing Irish records in an attempt to locate the grave of his famous great uncle Robert. In 1905, as part of that quest, he found the headless skeleton of a man in a Dublin cemetery, quite possibly St. Michan's, which was believed to be that of his heroic ancestor.

Finally, it is fitting to note that the Emmet family's strong ancestral and nationalist beliefs burned in young Thomas's breast as well. During his lifetime, Dr. Thomas Emmet supported Irish Fenian efforts in America, patronised the Irish Parliamentary Party's Home Rule efforts and became a friend to Patrick Pearse, the leader of the 1916 Dublin Easter Rebellion. On 15 September 1922, three years after his death, Dr. Emmet's body was laid to rest in Dublin's Glasnevin Cemetery. During the intervening years since his death, the British had refused to allow his body back into Ireland. It was only after the establishment of the Irish Free State's Provisional government, under the leadership of Michael Collins, that Ireland welcomed home another of its dead champions.

'TIS IRELAND, MY FREELAND

I raise my voice to the highlands,
To her hills and her valleys so grand;
'Tis Ireland, My Freeland I'm calling,
Come home and together we'll stand.

I think of the time of the ancients,
When Eireann was wild and so free;
When kings ruled the land of the Irish,
From the mountains to the shores of her seas.

Gaelic laws and their customs and culture,
All endured the hardships of time;
One thousand years and much longer,
An island, a freeland so fine.

Cuchulainn and Finn and dear Brian,
All warriors of fame and renown;
I long for their strength and their wisdom,
My homeland free and unbound.

Then the Normans rode in and they plundered,
They stole all the land and they cried...
"Ye Irish will live as we tell you,
And those that resist, they shall die."

Oh Strongbow, Queen Bess and old Cromwell,
They changed all the laws and made crimes
Out of living the ways that were Irish;
But proud Ireland survived through those times.

Finally, the people rose up in defiance,
Led by Tone and Emmet and Dwyer;
They had dreamt of their island unfettered,
But their rebellions just spawned England's ire.

From Parnell to the Easter Rebellion,
Brave Connolly and Pearse and the rest;
Lit the torch of hope and of freedom,
That still burns in many a breast.

Now the truce and the treaty are history,
And many have given their all
For an island, a freeland united;
Please God, help us and answer the call.

For I raise my voice to the highlands,
To her hills and her valleys so grand;
'Tis Ireland, My Freeland I'm calling,
Come home and united we'll stand.

A CHRISTMAS
HOMECOMING...

A CHRISTMAS
HOMECOMING...

Originally written in 1996, this piece was intended to honour the impending retirement of Galway's legendary shopkeeper Sonny Malloy and his wife Teddy. I also wanted to bring to mind some of the time-honoured Irish customs practised for decades. Like so much of today's Celtic-Tiger Ireland, life is changing and changing quickly. Lost in the rush to catch up and mimic the rest of the western world, the Emerald Isle is sadly throwing out the baby with the bathwater. Its amalgamation with the rest of the European Union and America contains the flux of both renaissance and corruption. Today, the draper's shop in Galway's High Street has been converted into a 'fashionable' pub!

Bits of this story were revised several times over the past seven years. A part of it was read on public radio in Cincinnati, Ohio at the end of 2000, while the 2001 version appeared in the December issue of the *Midwest Irish News*, published in Columbus, Ohio.

A CHRISTMAS HOMECOMING...Going home for Christmas is a special occasion for most people and a recent visit of mine is no exception. A wonderful kind of magical anticipation fills the air as my plane touches down in Dublin Town.

Though the Irish do not go in for all the exterior decorating Americans do, the Christmas spirit is visible everywhere. Shop windows shine brightly, trying to satisfy everyone's gift-giving urges. Candles glow in tall Georgian windows around the city's old squares. Public houses and restaurants are more crowded than ever...each filled with merrymakers lifting glasses of Guinness, mulled wine or Irish whiskey. More affluent diners sit by candlelight at linen-covered tables, feasting on roasted pheasant, grilled Connemara salmon or succulent Wicklow lamb. Turf fires blaze in little fireplaces while colourful paper crackers garnish most tables. The announcement of Christmas pudding graces the bottom of special holiday menus.

After my usual pilgrimage to Mass at St. Mary Pro-Cathedral followed by a short excursion to the seasonal Irish Christmas Craft Fair in the Rotunda Room at Mansion House, I head for Heuston Station. The evening train for the west of Ireland is soon leaving.

Sure all of the family is gone now, but old friends still remain. Happily so, the next ten days will be filled with the telling and re-telling of stories intermingled with visits to familiar timeworn places. Even the traditional arrival of the neighbouring Wren Boys is much anticipated, though today their song demands 50p or a punt instead of the odd penny or two.

On Christmas Eve a friend and I drive the narrow coast road down to a little village beside the gently rolling waters of the bay. We come to partake of some lovely fresh oysters, drink a few pints of the Liffey's finest stout and visit an old friend and his wife. After nearly sixty years of trading, their welcoming shop door will soon close for the last time. No more will the local village, farm and fisher folk enjoy the pleasures of sitting tall in the draper's well-worn chair as they bargain and buy from the couple who has served this community well for lo these many years.

All the locals know the shop's prices are slightly inflated. This allows a little leeway, permitting the fine art of 'give and take' to transpire. The final purchase price often depends on each participant's ability to size up the other. If the customer is likely to return again, a bob or two is magnanimously lopped off amid a flourish of words, nods and smiles. Upon observation, it is craft both buyer and seller seem to relish with much pleasure.

As for the draper's chair...as soon as 'the lady-of-the-house' enters the shop, my merchant friend, seizing the proper moment, slides the tall high-backed wooden chair under her backside. Now, settled comfortably at the raised counter, the woman can carefully examine her potential purchases, seated serenely so in regal repose just as if she were home beside her glowing hearth.

Like his father before him, the shopkeeper painstakingly pulls down an astonishing assortment of large, lovingly worn cardboard boxes. With great pride, he opens each one. Bales of woven flannel, striped grandfather shirts, woollen socks, old-fashioned cotton knickers and long johns, hand-knit jumpers and a generous assortment of footwear for all occasions are carefully paraded before the interested party. Soon the counter top is bedecked in a colourful display of inviting merchandise. Everything is thoughtfully examined, while the finer points of each item are politely debated.

At last, after a mutually agreeable price is reached, the items ready to change hands are dotingly set aside. With payment made, both the shopper and the draper seem to share a mutual sense of satisfaction so often missing in today's overly commercial, hurry-up world.

In a few months, however, the shop's shutters and metal gate will close for the last time. My friend and his wife will retire to enjoy a much deserved 'new life.' Sadly though, with their departure, another bit of old Ireland disappears. In its place emerges a new, more modern and increasingly plastic world that is rapidly replacing the one I have known and loved.

With the evening darkening down around us, my travelling companion and I drive out of the village. Facing for home, our hearts are filled with many a mixed feeling. In the evening's twilight, my thoughts recall the melancholy but sage observations of American writer Thomas Wolfe. Winding our way up from the Atlantic's rugged coastline, I know he was right...you can never go home again...not to the old place you once knew and loved in days gone by.

IT TAKES TWO
TO MAKE PEACE
WORK...

IT TAKES TWO TO MAKE
PEACE WORK...

Over the last two years, Northern Irish politics has experienced a continual series of ups and downs. Unless there are some significant breakthroughs in the months and years ahead, I am guessing things will continue to limp along much as they have since the signing of the Good Friday Peace Accord back in April 1998. The historic issues of political distrust and religious division run too deeply to be resolved overnight. Democracy accented with peace and justice for all is still a dream.

As of January, 2003, the Northern Irish Assembly is languishing under its fourth British government suspension since its inception three years ago (February, 2000; August, 2001; September, 2001 & October, 2002). On 1 July 2001, David Trimble finally made good his promise to resign as leader of his government's executive, but was re-elected the following November. The anti-agreement element within Mr. Trimble's Ulster Unionist Party continues to grow in number, causing him no end of leadership problems. During the last northern general election in June, 2001, more disheartened Protestant conservatives supported Reverend Ian Paisley's right-wing Democratic Unionist Party than previously. As a counterbalance, Sinn Fein received more nationalist votes than ever before. The citizenry in NI seems to be aligning themselves on either side of the divide rather than seeking some common ground.

The North has undergone other changes since the April, 1998 Agreement signing. Britain's Northern Irish Secretary Mo Mowlam, who played such an important part in the negotiating process, resigned in the autumn of 1999. Peter Mandelson followed her, but was replaced by John Reid in January, 2001. In November, 2002 Paul Murphy took over the reins as Britain's representative in the North from Reid. And so it goes... Northern Ireland is more likely to break a person than it is to make one.

In historic moves the Irish Republican Army verifiably decommissioned a large cache of weapons in October, 2001 and again in April, 2002. Last July, it also publicly acknowledged the grief of the families whose members it had killed during the last thirty years of guerrilla warfare. "We offer our sincere apologies and condolences to the families of noncombatants," an IRA spokesperson said. "There have been fatalities amongst combatants on all sides. We also acknowledge the grief and pain of their relatives," the republican organisation said in its apology.

In September, 2001 John Hume, the father of modern Northern Irish politics, resigned his twenty-two-year-old leadership post in the Social Democratic and Labour Party, citing ill health. Mr. Hume was replaced by Mark Durkin. Seamus Mallon, Hume's faithful lieutenant, also stepped down from the Assembly and from his SDLP leadership position.

The streets of NI continue to be beset with violence as sectarian paraders persist in demanding their right to march down the Queen's highways regardless of who lives along them or the damage they inflict.

Illegal, quasi-paramilitary gangs roam through selected neighbourhoods of the North in ever increasing numbers, beating, shooting, and on occasions, killing those they begrudge or those who oppose them. All the while, racketeering and drug-related criminal activity grows more prevalent. Failure on the part of many to deal with this general climate of growing crime and violence has become a major stumbling block in the successful implementation of the Good Friday Agreement.

There are also other major issues on the table that must be resolved before the long-sought nationalist principles of equality, inclusion and democracy can be achieved in the Six Counties. These issues include the matters of loyalist and republican weapons decommissioning, continued police reform, the demilitarisation of Northern Irish society from both a British army as well as a paramilitary standpoint, and a stabilisation of devolved governmental institutions. Additionally, Dublin's Irish government must become more vocal in making certain that Westminster honours all of its Good Friday pledges. Yes, there is much to do before Northern Ireland can settle down and make peace with itself, as communal dislike continues to prevent both unionists and nationalists from meaningful discussions held in the absense of fear and countercharge.

Finally, just to let everyone know how far things have to go, David Trimble caused a mild uproar last March when he called for a referendum on whether NI should remain part of the United Kingdom at this spring's 2003-Assembly election. He concluded his surprising remarks by describing the Republic of Ireland as a "pathetic, sectarian, mono-ethnic and mono-cultural" society while still strongly demanding that the IRA continue its decommissioning process.

Ah sure, you cannot blame the man for confusing the Republic with the North. He was probably just having another bad day...frustrated by the lack of progress back home, no doubt!

I try to remain optimistic about the future of the Six Counties. Peace and justice will come to NI when both unionist and nationalist leaders seek to truly establish a fair and democratic government in the North. To do so, however, they must be willing to change the century-old practice of fostering and tolerating sectarianism and distrust.

Based on events of the recent past, it seems that Sinn Fein is knowingly modifying its political stance while the Agreement rejectionists are deliberately hardening theirs. Unfortunately, David Trimble and most certainly Ian Paisley have become Northern Ireland's political dinosaurs. Trouble stalks the horizon on their watch.

As a counterbalance, the IRA is laying down its guns and honouring its ceasefire with renewed courage and conviction. Sinn Fein's leadership, in the persons of Gerry Adams and Martin McGuinness, must be respected, listened to and trusted. No good can come of it, if they are isolated and threatened.

A brighter tomorrow will dawn in Northern Ireland when its two traditionally conflicting communities begin acknowledging their many similarities and honouring their unique differences. When they finally begin to trust one another and to forgive without rancour. When inclusiveness rather than exclusiveness becomes a valued commodity. That will be the day when hope is truly reborn in Ireland. So please God, help us deliver a nation of peace to the children of our tomorrow. They and Ireland deserve nothing less.

THE WINDS ARE SINGING FREEDOM…

THE WINDS ARE SINGING FREEDOM...

By Tommy Makem

There's a time laid out for laughing
There's a time laid out to weep
There's a time laid out for sowing
And a time laid out to reap
There's a time to love your brother
There's a time for hate to cease
You must sow the seeds of justice
To reap the fruits of peace.

And the winds are singing freedom
They sing it everywhere
They sing it on the mountainside
And in the city square
They sing of a new day dawning
When our people will be free
Come and join their song of freedom
Let it ring from sea to sea.

ABOUT THE ARTIST
EDMUND SULLIVAN...

Irish-American by birth, raised on the streets of the Bronx and educated by Fordham's Jesuits, artist Edmund Sullivan regards the west coast of Ireland as his spiritual home. It has been his primary artistic subject matter for thirty years.

Mr. Sullivan's work has been exhibited in dozens of galleries. He has been honoured in *American Artist* magazine and exhibited in the Irish-American Heritage Museum, Cairo, New York. He has received countless distinguished awards from cities and states, and his work has been featured in Irish movies and television. Through his many appearances promoting Irish art and culture, Mr. Sullivan has raised hundreds of thousands of dollars for Irish charitable organisations by donating framed prints for fund-raising efforts.

Currently, he is in the process of converting part of his studio into a gallery. So the next time you are near Sandy Hook, Connecticut call in and say hello.

To contact Edmund Sullivan, to request a catalogue or to order one of his many wonderful paintings or prints of Ireland, go to ***www.edmundsullivan.com*** or telephone 800.445.8734.

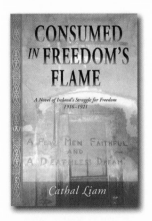